AF434090

100 EXERCISES AND GAMES for FUTSAL INITIATION

José Ignacio Pérez Sánchez
Jaime Cruz Solano
Alicia Solís Rodríguez

Title: 100 EXERCISES AND GAMES FOR FUTSAL INITIATION

Authors: José Ignacio Pérez Sánchez, Jaime Cruz Solano, Alicia Solís Rodríguez

Translation: Alicia Solís Rodríguez

Publisher: WANCEULEN S.L.
Collection: WANCEULEN EDITORIAL DEPORTIVA
Series of books: WANCEULEN FÚTBOL FORMATIVO

ISBN (paper book): 978-84-18486-92-0
ISBN (Ebook): 978-84-18486-93-7

LEGAL DEPOSIT REGISTRATION NUMBER: SE 2131-2020

Printed in Spain: 2020.

WANCEULEN S.L.
C/ Cristo del Desamparo y Abandono, 56 - 41006 Sevilla
Dirección web: www.wanceuleneditorial.com y www.wanceulen.com
Email: info@wanceuleneditorial.com

ÍNDICE

INTRODUCTION

This title belongs to a collection of games and exercises for the different sport technicians and monitors in which, each of them are offered 100 games and exercises for their training and teaching. This collection covers up a bibliographic gap about the teaching-learning sports process.

The suggested activities can be applied directly. In order to apply them to the different levels of teaching and/or training according to the groups we are working with, we only have to apply the appropriate changes we consider suitable: adjust the execution speed, emphasize or mitigate the difficulty of the actions, restrict or increase the number of limitation rules, restrict or increase the space and distance...

The included activities are conceived under a comprehensive vision of training developing all the technical-tactical contents with the current guidelines that regulate the teaching-learning processes of sports activities and that seek the simultaneous improvement of technical, tactical, physical aspects and psychological.

Methodologically, these activities offer a practice close to the real competition situation in which the internal relationship processes, typical of sports, are established with the fundamental objective that the player with the fundamental objective that the player encourages and enhances thinking and tactical abilities, based on continuous decision making.

All the activities are presented in a graphic representation marked by clarity, in a way that their initial structure and dynamics are observable at first sight. Each of these graphic representations is accompanied by an explanatory sheet, in which the main and secondary objectives, the technical-tactical means used, and the organizational characteristics are explained: number of players, size of the field, material used and activity time.

Practical material to develop the training and preparation sessions for all ages and levels.

The sports technician in training stages, and the physical education teacher, have always demanded useful works with games and practical activities to enliven the session, and that collect the specific aspects necessary for correct motor training and adequate performance in sports practice and collect the specific aspects necessary for a right motor training and adequate achievement in sports practice.

For inexperienced technicians it represents a simplification when it comes to prepare the daily lessons. And for experienced technicians it represents a base on which they can build their daily work for the improvement of both generic and specific skills, with the contribution of their own experience.

Therefore, in this work we have included highly selected activities from the wide existing repertoire, with the aim of providing a real proposal that is easy to put into practice, avoiding to create a manual full of variants or activities of doubtful efficacy.

INTRODUCTION TO FUTSAL

Futsal or Futsal is a collaboration-opposition sport (socio motor sport), characterized by its high motor commitment in the player constant adaptation to a changing and dynamic environment, with time deficit and space to notice, make decisions and carry out the actions that provide solutions to the game.

GAME FACTORS

- Game space: 40x20 track where the game sense is determined by each of the two goals.
- Game involvement: it is a 5x5 game with constant exchange options with other players who jump into the pitch from the bench, what revitalises participation and intensity, and in which

involvement and effect on the game of the 5 players participating per team is constant and meaningful.

- Main component: it is the mobile, the ball and, therefore, the game is conditioned by the fact that whether it is in possession or not.
- Playing time: it is conditioned to the ball which is in the game. It is usually two halves of 20 minutes, although it varies in certain competitions.
- Regulations: they regulate the game.

Game aims

- Attack: ball preservation -game improvement- finalisation/score a goal.
- Defense: ball recovery -avoid game progression- avoid the goal.
- Conditional abilities and motor communication: physical base of the action.
- Technique: execution of the different game actions.
- Tactic: combination of actions which, through the use of available means and the analysis of the situations, try to manage the specific game aim.

Most relevant aspects and factors of the game:

- Collaboration-opposition sport, dynamic and intense.
- Space and time deficit.
- Highly perceptive-decisional and, therefore, tactical-cognitive component.
- Support in the physical and technical aspects for the execution of the game actions.
- The main objective of the game is, evidently, to score a goal.
- The most decisive technique gestures are the control, the pass and the shot to the goal.

- It is a game which requires high levels of accuracy and speed, in the decisions making, with the suitable motor physic and technical.

Physically, it stands out for sporadic efforts of high intensity of short or medium duration which require enough rest periods and a basic work which produces optimal levels of strength and resistance to speed to maintain an effective rhythm.

It has an eminently tactic component, given its constant interrelation. This type of collaboration-opposition relationship is produced with or without the ball, that is to say, in any of the attack/defense game stages and in a simultaneous way. Nevertheless, it is sometimes necessary to attack against an organised and positioned defense, it turns to the building of the attack which could be elaborated or more direct.

The actions to stopped ball, corner, sideline or foul are especially important in Futsal, since, due to the goals proximity, they are actions with great possibilities to end in goal.

The main positions are: goalkeeper, closing, branch, centre. As in most of the sport specialities, there are versatile player called universal players and some specialist players with a high command of some specific skills.

FORMATION STAGES

The evolutionary stages of the young futsal player on his formation process, is also very similar to the rest of sports collective specialities and could be the followings:

- Initiation: includes from 6 to 10 years old, a period in which the player becomes familiar with the game in an organised way.
- Development: includes from 11 to 14 years old, a period in which the player begins to understand the game in an organised and structured way.

- Specialised formation: includes from 15 to 16 years old, a period in which the player begins to make use of the learnt tactic in previous stages and progress in tactic aspects.
- Perfection: includes from 17 to 18 years old, a period in which the learnt in previous stages is improved and consolidated, with a more complex organisation tactic.
- High performance: includes from 18 years old, getting stuck into the efficiency stage where the player has fully developed the high competition demands.

The texts in this section has been summarized, adapted, simplified and modified, from contents included in the "Manual de la UEFA para Entrenadores de Fútbol Sala" / UEFA manual for Futsal trainers" in its 2017 edition, elaborated by José Venancio López Hierro.

SIMBOLOGY

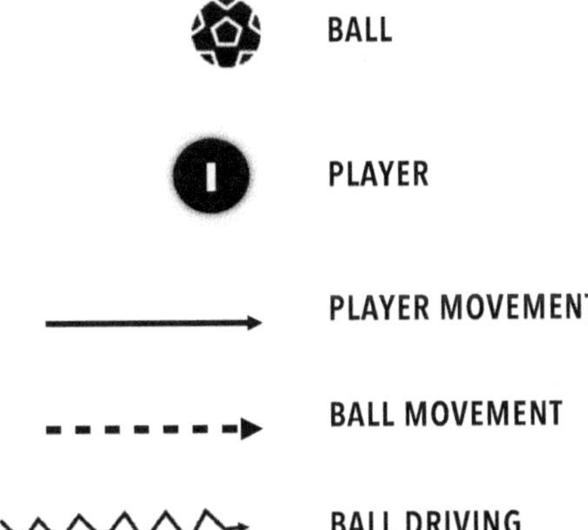

100 SELECTED EXERCISES AND GAMES FOR THE INITIATION OF FUTSAL

Exercise N° 1	Main Objective	To improve the ball control
	Secondary Objectives	To improve the pass
Tactical-Technical Means	pass-reception, support and shifting	
Players	4 (3 attacker x 1 defense)	Field	8m x 8m x 8m (triangle)
Material	Cones, ball	Time	8'
Explanation		

Game 3:1 with the 3 attackers located in the triangle corners and the defense tries to recover the ball.

It is compulsory played two touches.

Observations	It is compulsory played two touches. (control-pass).

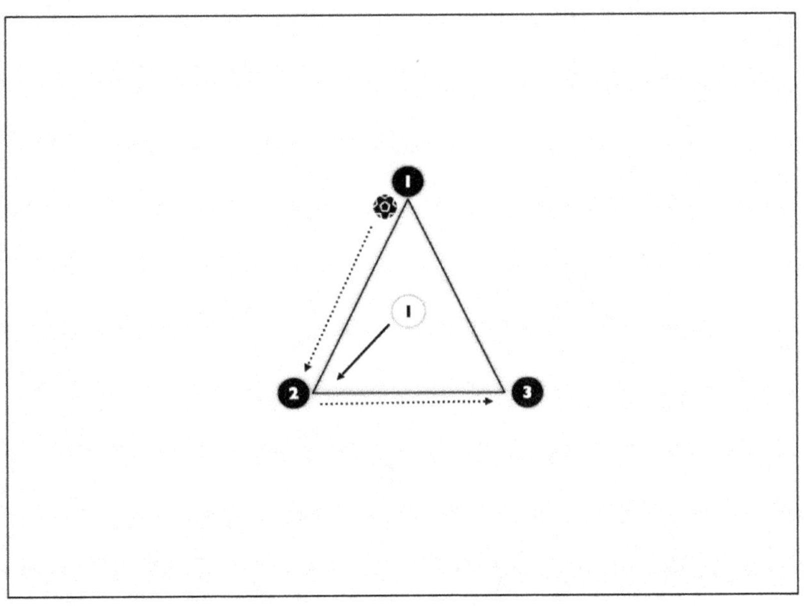

Exercise Nº 2	Main Objective	To improve the ball control
	Secondary Objectives	To improve the pass
Tactical-Technical Means	Lose the mark, pass-reception, support, shifting	
Players	6 (4 attacker x 2 defense)	Field	10m x 10m
Material	Cones, ball	Time	8'
Explanation			

Game 4:2 with 4 attackers located in the four square edges, being able to move laterally for each side to give support and the 2 defense try to recover the ball.

Observations	It is compulsory played two touches. (control-pass).

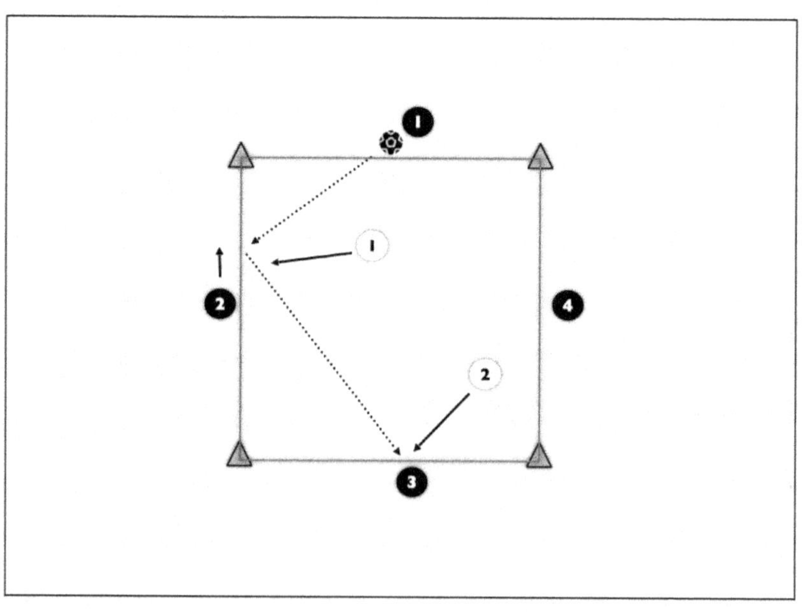

Exercise N° 3	Main Objective	To improve the ball control
	Secondary Objectives	To improve the pass

Tactical-Technical Means	Lose the mark, pass-reception, support, shifting		
Players	6 (2 teams of 2 players+ 2 all-rounders)	Field	10m x 10m
Material	Cones, ball	Time	3 x 3'

Explanation

Game 2:2+2 all-rounders who play with the team in ball possesion and support from the inner field. The defense try to steal the ball to the other team.

Observations	Every 3' change the all-rounder It is compulsory played two touches. (control-pass).

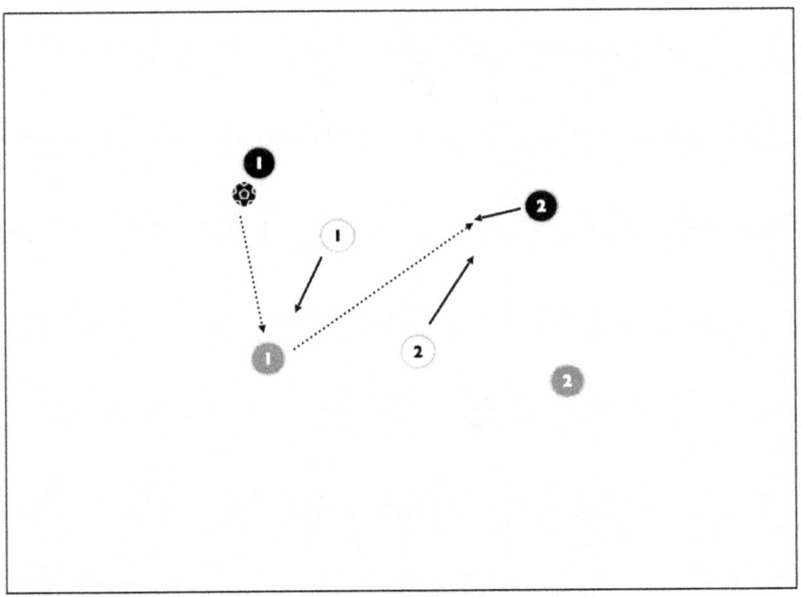

Exercise Nº 4	Main Objective	To improve the ball control
	Secondary Objectives	To improve the pass
Tactical-Technical Means	Lose the mark, pass-reception, support, shifting	
Players	10 (2 teams of 5 players)	Field	20m x 20m
Material	Cones, ball	Time	8'
Explanation			

Game 5:5 the team in possession of the ball get one point for each player control, after which they will get with the ball possession.

Observations	It is compulsory played two touches. (control-pass).

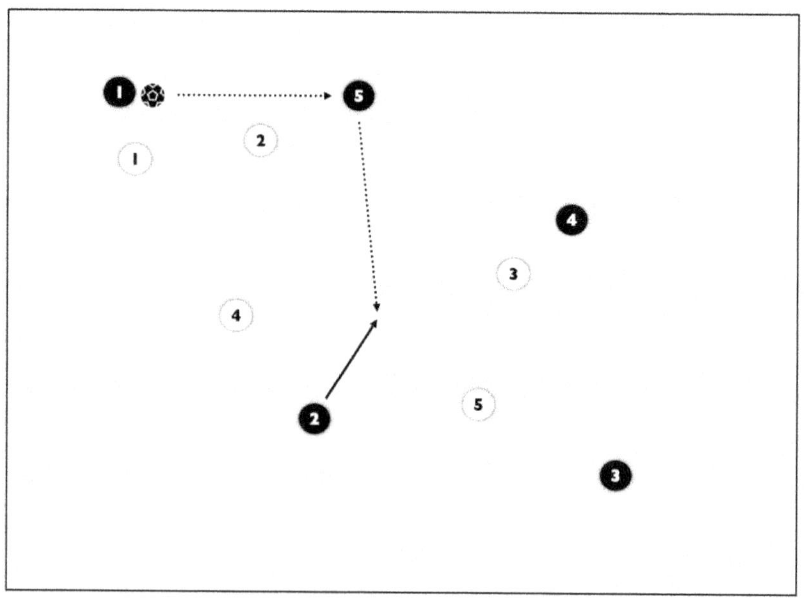

Exercise N° 5	Main Objective	To improve the ball control
	Secondary Objectives	To improve the pass
Tactical-Technical Means	Lose the mark, pass-reception, support, shifting	
Players	10 (2 teams of 5 players)	Field	20m x 20m (zone 10m x 10m)
Material	Cones, ball	Time	8'
Explanation		

Game 5:5 is demarcated in a central zone. The team with ball possession gets one point each time a player controls the ball inside the central zone, after which they will get with the ball possession.

Observations	It is compulsory played two touches. (control-pass).

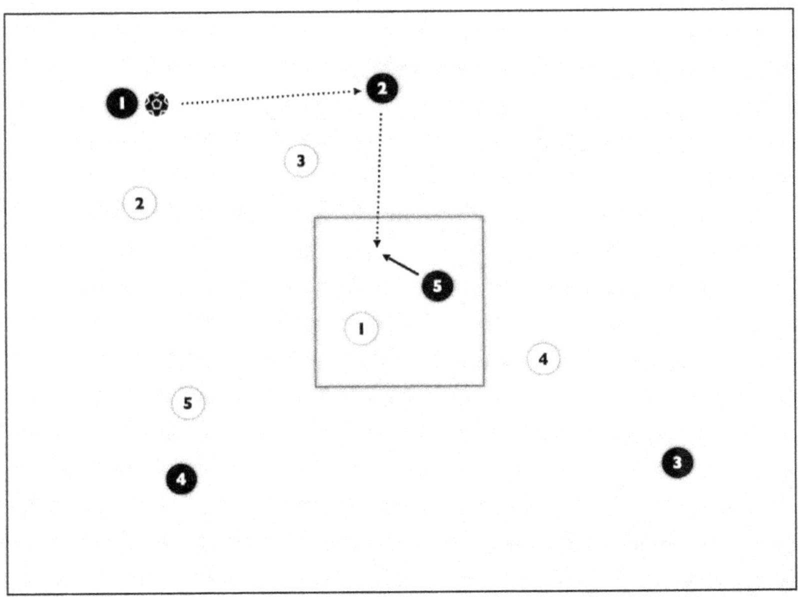

Exercise Nº 6	Main Objective	To improve the ball control
	Secondary Objectives	To improve the pass
Tactical-Technical Means	Lose the mark, pass-reception, support, shifting	

Players	10 (2 teams of 5 players)	Field	20m x 20m
Material	Cones, ball	Time	8'

Explanation

Game 5:5 the team with the ball possession is obliged to play with the following sequences of passes: 3 short + 1 long, if they achieve it, they score 1 point and keep ball possession.

Observations	It is compulsory played two touches. (control-pass).

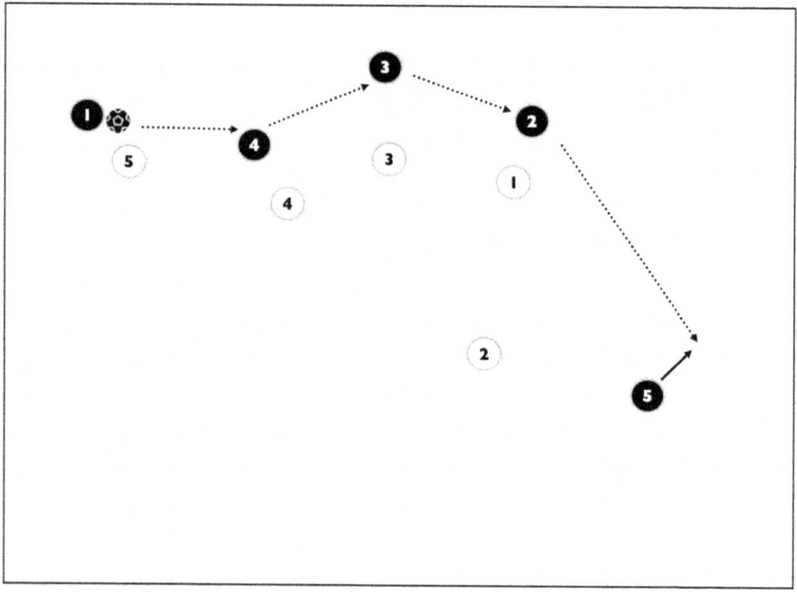

Exercise N° 7	Main Objective	To improve the ball control
	Secondary Objectives	To improve the pass
Tactical-Technical Means	Lose the mark, pass-reception, support, shifting	
Players	10 (2 teams of 5 players)	Field	30m x 20m (3 small goals of 2m)
Material	Cones, ball	Time	8'

Explanation

Game 5:5. 3 goals are placed in the field (see graphic). The team with ball possession scores 1 point each time the players achieve to control a pass throughout any of the goals after which they continue with the ball possession.

Observations	It is compulsory played two touches. (control-pass).

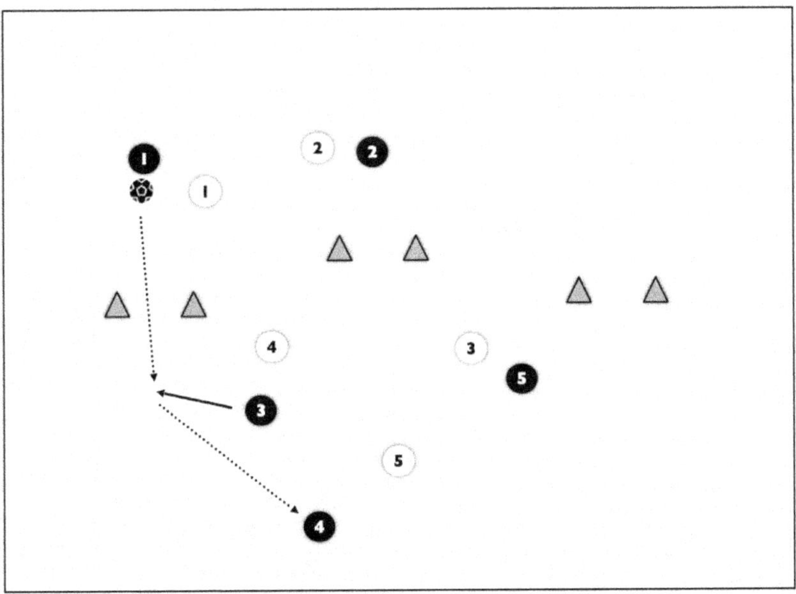

Exercise Nº 8	Main Objective	To improve the ball control
	Secondary Objectives	To improve the pass and lose the mark
Tactical-Technical Means	Lose the mark, pass-reception, support, shifting	
Players	5 teams (2 teams of 2 players +1 defense all-rounder)	Field	12m x 12m
Material	Cones, ball	Time	6 x 2'
Explanation		

Game 2:2+1 all-rounder who goes with the defense team (see graphic). The attacker team should try to keep the ball possession.

Observations	Change the all-rounders every 2' It is compulsory played 2-3 touches.

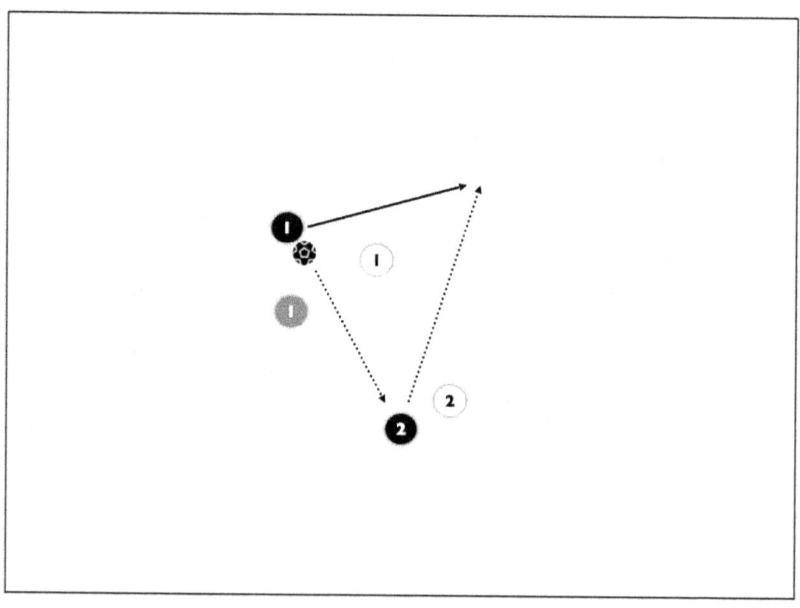

Exercise N° 9	Main Objective	To improve the ball conducting
	Secondary Objectives	To improve the pass and control

Tactical-Technical Means	Pass-reception, support, conducting, ball management		
Players	6 (2 teams of 2 players +2 all-rounder)	Field	12m x 12m
Material	Cones, ball	Time	3 x 4'

Explanation

Game 2:2+2 all-rounders who go with the ball possession team and who support from the inner playing field. The player with the ball possession has to give four touches to the ball (conducting) before passing the ball.

Observations	Change the all-rounders every 4'.

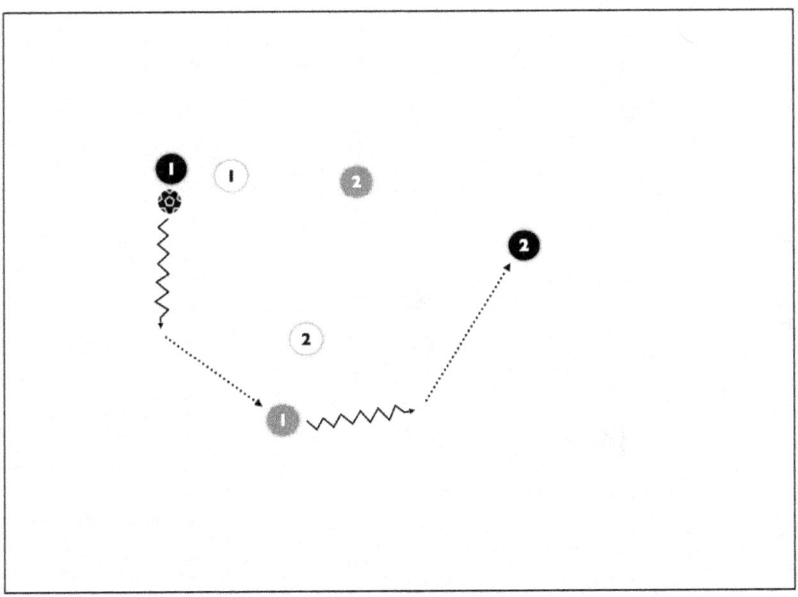

Exercise N° 10	Main Objective	To improve the ball conducting
	Secondary Objectives	To improve the pass and control
Tactical-Technical Means	Pass-reception, support, conducting, ball management	
Players	10 (2 teams of 4 players +2 all-rounder)	Field	30m x 20m
Material	Cones, ball	Time	5 x 2'

Explanation

Game 4:4+2 all-rounders who go with the ball possession team and who support from the inner playing field. The player with the ball possession has to give four touches to the ball (conducting) before passing the ball.

Observations	Change the all-rounders every 2'.

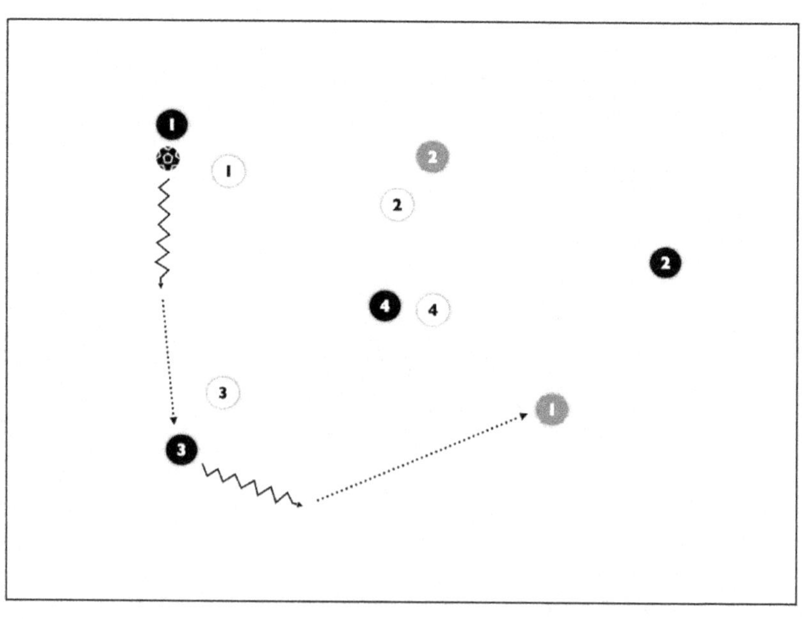

Exercise N° 11	Main Objective	To improve the ball conducting
	Secondary Objectives	To improve the pass and lose the mark

Tactical-Technical Means	Pass-reception, support, conducting, ball management		
Players	10 (2 teams of 4 players +2 all-rounder)	Field	30m x 20m + 4 2m x 2m squares
Material	Cones, ball	Time	5 x 2'

Explanation

Game 4:4+2 all-rounders who go with the ball possession team and who support from the inner playing field. 4 squares are placed in the field (see graphic). The team with the ball possession scores a point every time a player receives the ball in the inner square, taking it out to one of the triangles, whereupon they will continue with the ball possession.

Observations	Change the all-rounders every 2'.

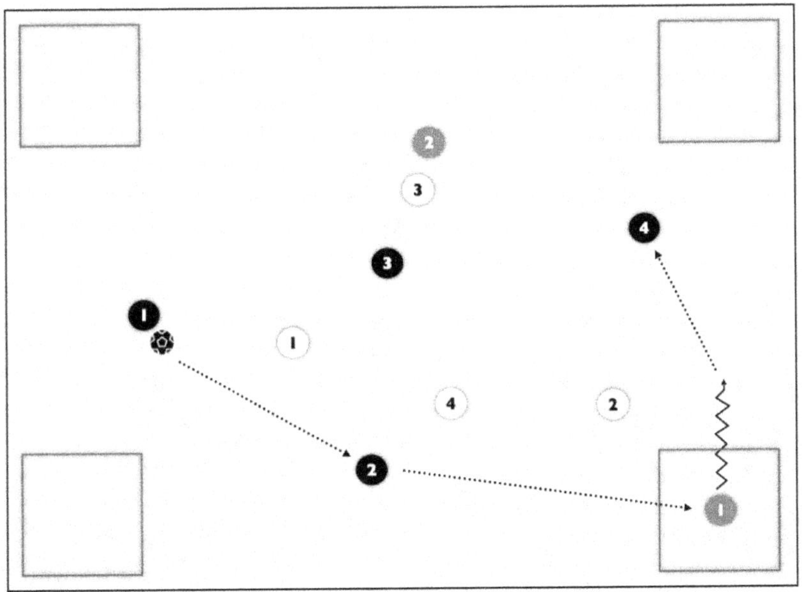

Exercise Nº 12	Main Objective	To improve the ball conducting
	Secondary Objectives	To improve the pass and lose the mark
Tactical-Technical Means	Pass-reception, support, conducting, ball management	
Players	10 (2 teams of 5 players)	Field	30m x 20m
Material	Cones, ball	Time	8'
Explanation		

Game 5:5 the player with the ball possession has to give as minimum 4 touches to the ball (conducting) before passing the ball.

Observations

Exercise N° 13	Main Objective	To improve the ball conducting
	Secondary Objectives	To improve the pass and lose the mark

Tactical-Technical Means	Pass-reception, support, conducting, ball management		
Players	10 (2 teams of 5 players)	Field	30m x 20m (zone 10m x 10m)
Material	Cones, ball	Time	8'

Explanation

Game 5:5 an inner field zone is marked (see graphic). The team with the ball possession scores a point every time a player receives the ball in the inner marked zone and when is able to take it out, whereupon they will continue with the ball possession.

Observations	It is not allowed to stay in the marked zone for more than 10'.

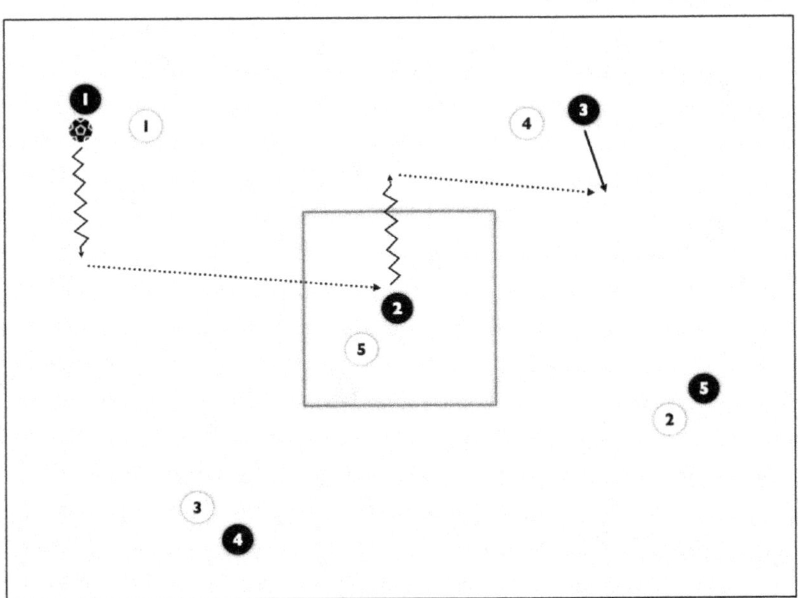

Exercise N° 14	Main Objective	To improve the ball conducting
	Secondary Objectives	To improve the pass and lose the mark
Tactical-Technical Means	Pass-reception, support, conducting, ball management	
Players	10 (2 teams of 5 players)	Field	30m x 20m (4 small goals of 2m)
Material	Cones, ball	Time	8'
Explanation			

Game 5:5, two 2m goals are placed. Each team attack and defend two goals (see graphic). The team with the ball possession scores a goal each time a player pierces to one of the protected goals by the rival, whereupon they will continue with the ball possession.

Observations	Goals can be crossed in both directions.

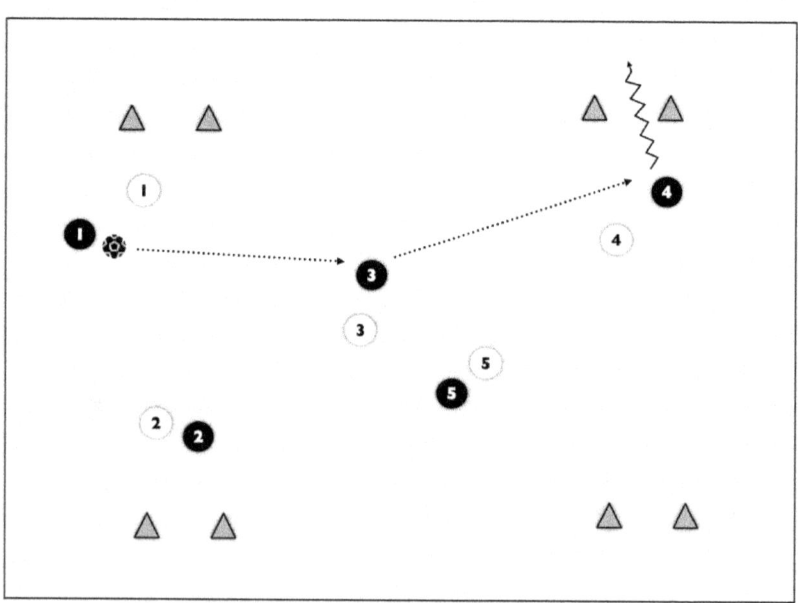

Exercise N° 15	Main Objective	To improve the ball conducting
	Secondary Objectives	To improve the pass and lose the mark

Tactical-Technical Means	Pass-reception, support, conducting, ball management		
Players	10 (2 teams of 5 players)	Field	30m x 20m (4 wide goals of 2m)
Material	Cones, ball	Time	8'
Explanation			

Game 5:5, two 20m wide goals are placed in the field. Each team attack and defend two goals (see graphic). The team with the ball possession scores a goal each time a player pierces to one of the protected goals by the rival, whereupon they will continue with the ball possession.

Observations	Goals can be crossed in both directions.

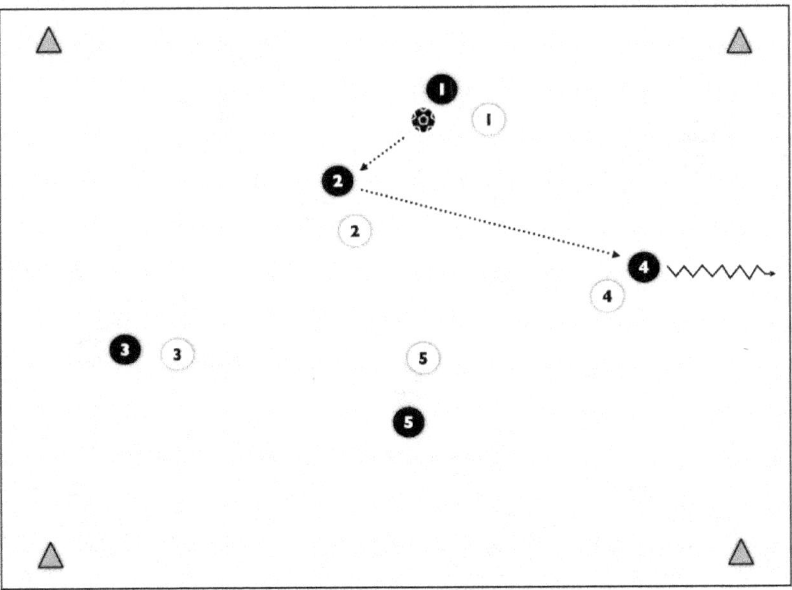

Exercise N° 16	Main Objective	To improve the ball conducting
	Secondary Objectives	To improve the pass and lose the mark
Tactical-Technical Means	Pass-reception, support, conducting, ball management	
Players	10 (2 teams of 5 players)	Field	30m x 20m (3 goals of 3m)
Material	Cones, ball	Time	8'
Explanation			

Game 5:5, three 30m wide goals are placed in the field. Each team attack and defend three neutral goals (see graphic). The team with the ball possession scores a goal each time a player pierces to one of the protected goals by the rival, whereupon they will continue with the ball possession.

Observations	Goals can be crossed in both directions.

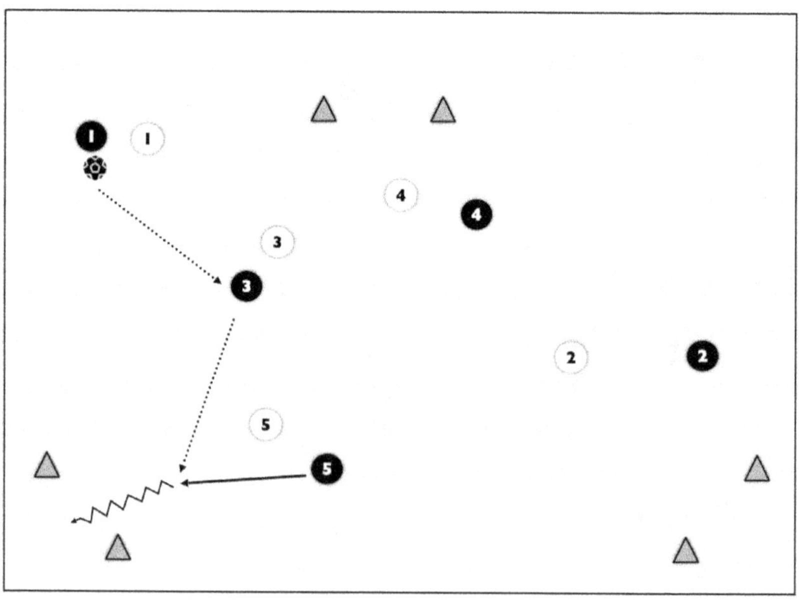

Exercise N° 17	Main Objective	To improve the ball conducting
	Secondary Objectives	To improve the pass and lose the mark

Tactical-Technical Means	Pass-reception, support, conducting, ball management		
Players	6 (2 teams of 2 players + 2 defense all-rounders)	Field	12m x 12m
Material	Cones, ball	Time	3 x 4'

Explanation

Game 2:2+2 defense all-rounders who help from the inner playing field. The player with the ball possession has to give 4 touches to the ball (conducting), before passing the ball.

Observations	Change the all-rounders every 4'.

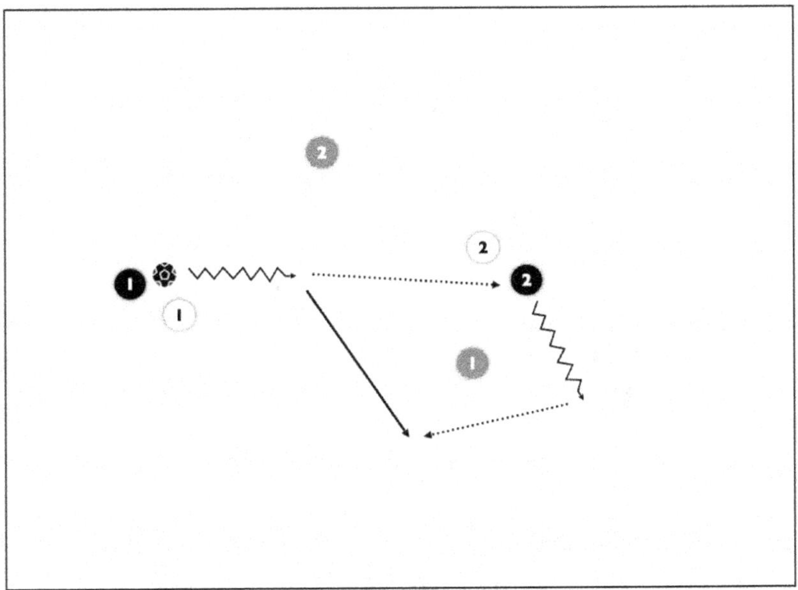

Exercise N° 18	Main Objective	To improve the ball conducting
	Secondary Objectives	To improve the occupation and the creation of areas.
Tactical-Technical Means	Pass-reception, support, conducting, ball management	
Players	10 (2 teams of 4 players + 2 defense all-rounders)	Field: 30m x 20m
Material	Cones, ball	Time: 5 x 2'
Explanation		

Game 4:4+2 defense all-rounders who help from the inner playing field. The player with the ball possession has to give 4 touches to the ball (conducting), before passing the ball.

Observations	Change the all-rounders every 2'.

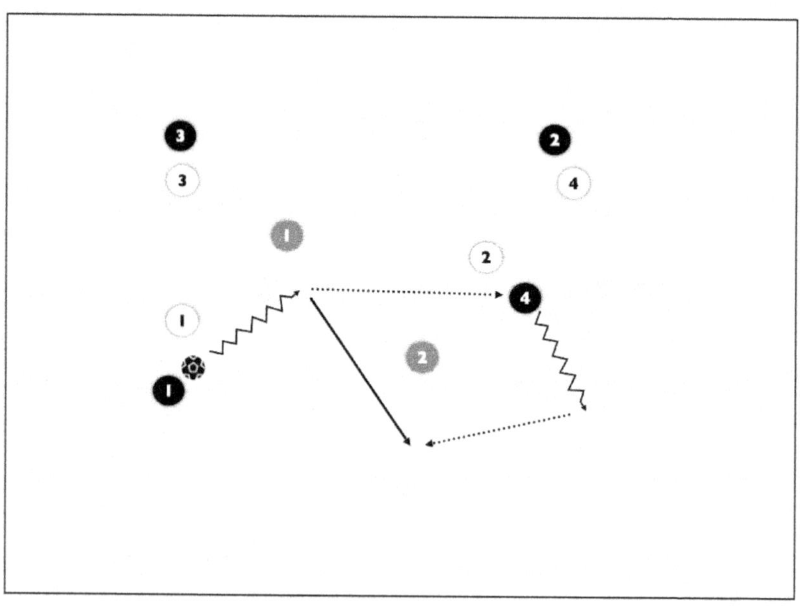

Exercise Nº 19	Main Objective	To improve the dribbling and feint
	Secondary Objectives	To improve the positional attack
Tactical-Technical Means	Dribbling, feint, conducting, ball management	
Players	9 (3 couples 1:1+3 all-rounders)	Field: 25m x 15m (2 marked zones of 5m x 7m)
Material	Cones y balls	Time: 6 x 1'

Explanation

Game   1:1+3 all-rounders (3 groups) which go with the ball possession. 2 marked zones are situated in the playing field, each player attacks and defends one of the marked zones (see graphic). The team with the ball possession (2:1) to score a goal, one of the players has to faint to his opponent and cross the marked zone protected by him whereupon they will continue with the ball possession.

Observations	Change the all-rounders every 2'.

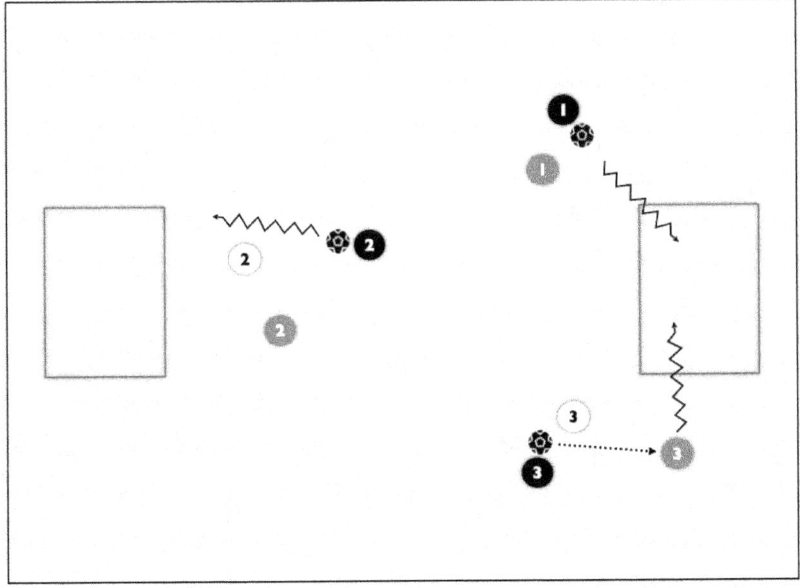

Exercise N° 20	Main Objective	To improve the dribbling and feint
	Secondary Objectives	To improve the positional attack
Tactical-Technical Means	dribbling , feint, conducting, ball management	
Players	9 (3 couples 1:1+3 all-rounders)	Field	25m x 15m (2 goals of 12m)
Material	Cones y balls	Time	6 x 1'

Explanation

Game 1:1+1 all-rounders (3 groups) which go with the ball possession. 2 wide goals of 12m are placed in the playing field, each player attacks and defends one wide goal (see graphic). The team with the ball possession (2:1) to score a goal, one of the players has to dribble to his opponent and cross the marked zone protected by him whereupon they will continue with the ball possession.

Observations	Change the all-rounders every 2'.

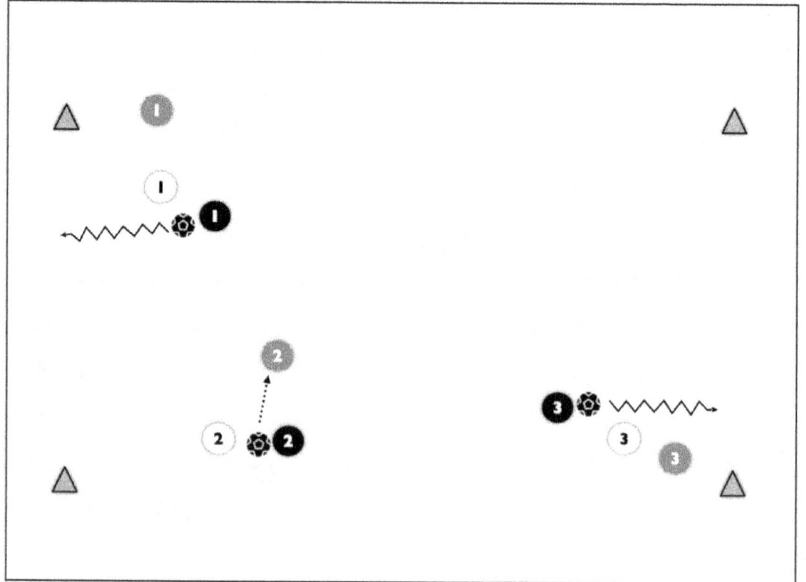

Exercise N° 21	Main Objective	To improve the dribbling and feint
	Secondary Objectives	To improve the positional attack
Tactical-Technical Means	dribbling , feint, conducting, ball management	
Players	9 (3 couples 1:1+3 all-rounders)	Field	25m x 20m (2 squares of 2m x 2m)
Material	Cones y balls	Time	6 x 1'

Explanation
Game   1:1+1 all-rounders (3 groups) which go with the ball possession. 4 squares are situated in the playing field, each player attacks and defends 2 of the squares (see graphic). The team with the ball possession (2:1) scores a point each time a player dribbles to his direct opponent and goes through one of the defended squares, whereupon they will continue with the ball possession.

Observations	Change the all-rounders every 1'.

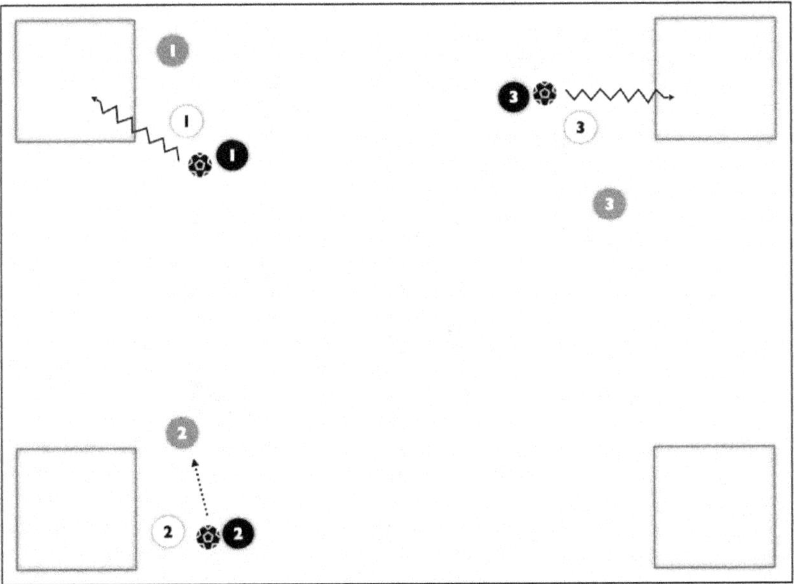

Exercise N° 22	Main Objective	To improve the dribbling and feint
	Secondary Objectives	To improve the positional attack
Tactical-Technical Means	dribbling, feint, conducting, ball management	
Players	12 (2 teams of 4 players + 4 all-rounders)	Field	20m x 20m (the field is divided into 4 zones of 10m x 10m)
Material	Cones y balls	Time	2 x 2'

Explanation

Game 4:4+4 which go with the ball possession. The playing field is divided into 4 marked zones, each team has a player in each zone (see graphic). The player with the ball possession has to dribble his direct opponent before passing the ball to another zone, whereupon the possession of the ball would be changed.

Observations	Change the all-rounders every 2'. The players cannot go out from his zone.

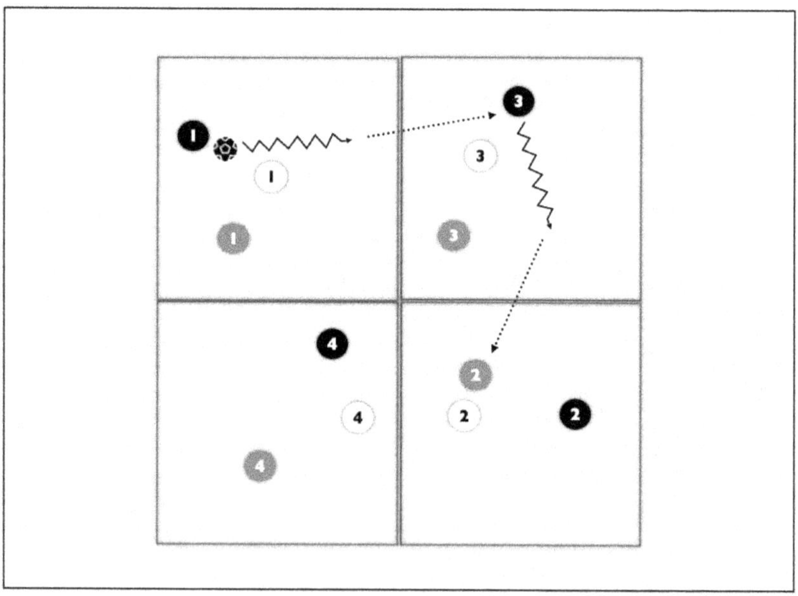

Exercise N° 23	Main Objective	To improve the dribbling and feint
	Secondary Objectives	To improve the positional attack
Tactical-Technical Means	dribbling, feint, conducting, ball management	
Players	9 (3 couples 1:1+3 all-rounders)	Field	25m x 20m (2 squares of 2m x 3m)
Material	Cones y balls	Time	6 x 1'

Explanation
Game 1:1+1 which go with the ball possession (3 groups). 2 marked zones of 2m x 2m are placed in the playing field (see graphic). The team with the ball possession to score a goal, one of the players has to dribble to his opponent and cross the marked zone protected by him whereupon they will continue with the ball possession.

Observations	Change the all-rounders every 1'.

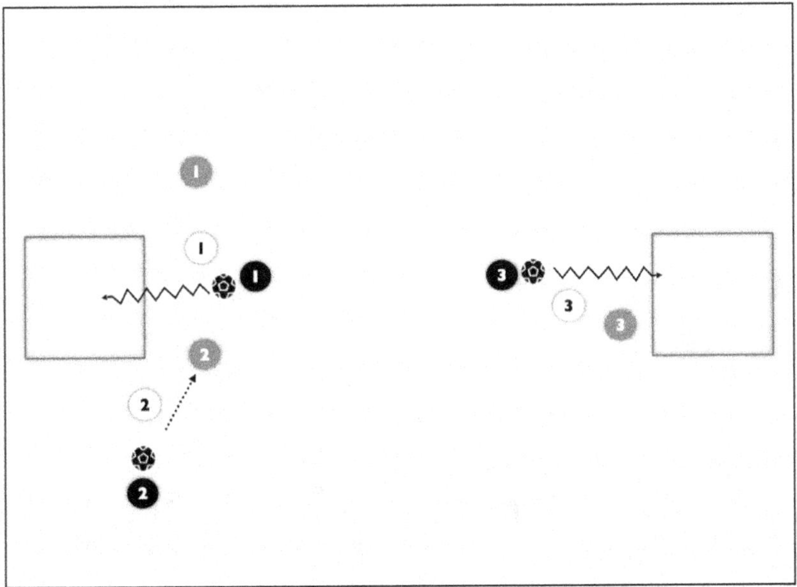

Exercise N° 24	Main Objective	To improve the dribbling and feint
	Secondary Objectives	To improve the offensive attack
Tactical-Technical Means	dribbling, feint, conducting, ball management	
Players	10 (5 couples of 1:1)	Field	25m x 15m (6 goals of 2m)
Material	Cones y balls	Time	6 x 1'
Explanation			

Game 1:1 (5 couples) 6 small goals of 2m are placed in the field. Each player attacks and defends 3 small goals (see graphic). The player with the ball possession to score a goal, one of the players has to dribble to his direct opponent and cross one of the defended goals, whereupon the ball possession will be changed.

Observations

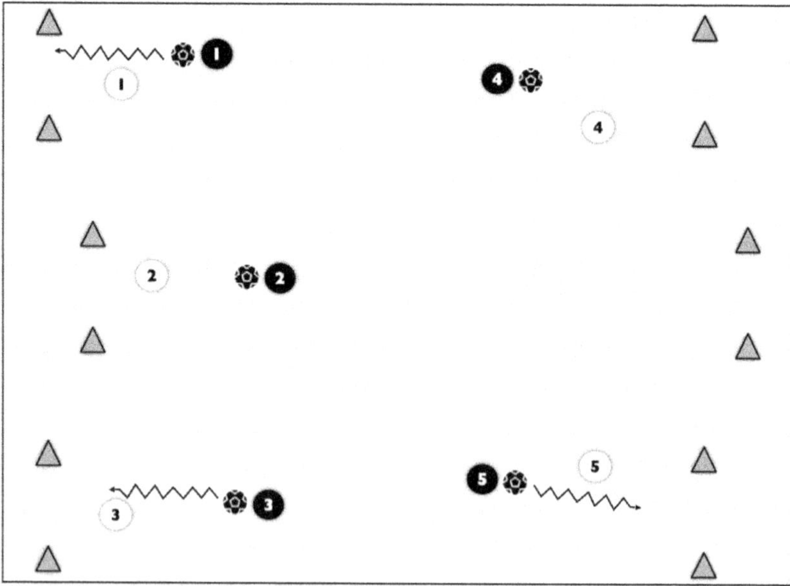

Exercise N° 25	Main Objective	To improve the dribbling and feint
	Secondary Objectives	To improve the offensive attack
Tactical-Technical Means	dribbling, feint, conducting, ball management	
Players	12 (5 couples of 1:1+2 goalkeepers)	Field	20m x 15m (2 wide goals of 12m)
Material	Cones y balls	Time	6 x 1'

Explanation

Game 1:1 (5 couples) 2 wide goals of 12m are placed in the playing field. Each player attacks and defends one wide goal (see graphic). The player with the ball possession to score a goal, one of the players has to dribble to his direct opponent and cross one of the goals defended by a goalkeeper, whereupon the ball possession will be changed.

Observations	If the goalkeeper catch the ball, he will deliver it to the defense.

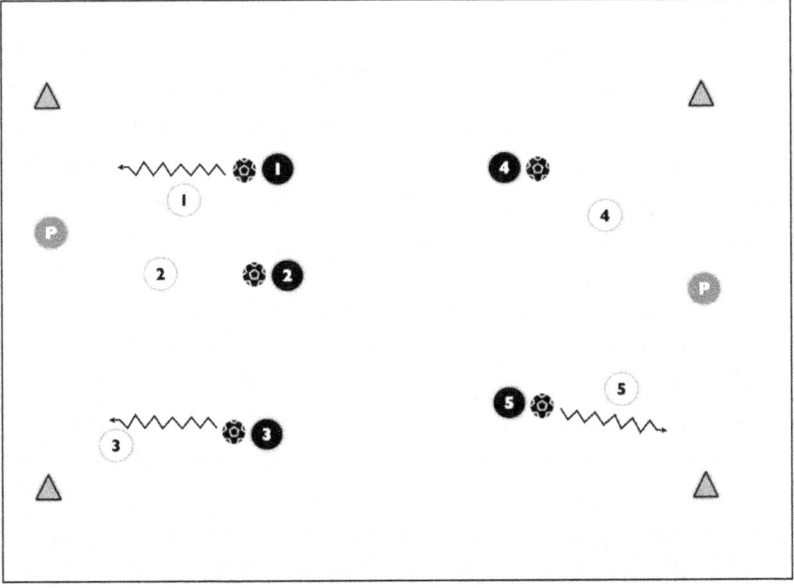

Exercise N° 26	Main Objective	To improve the dribbling and feint
	Secondary Objectives	To improve the offensive attack
Tactical-Technical Means		dribbling , feint, shot, conducting, ball management
Players	12 (5 couples of 1:1)	Field	20m x 15m (2 goals of 3m)
Material	Cones y balls	Time	6 x 1'
Explanation		

Game   1:1 (5 couples) 2 goals are placed in the playing field. Each player attacks and defends one smallgoal (see graphic). The player with the ball possession to score a goal, one of the players has to dribble to his direct opponent and shoot to the small goal defended by the opponent, whereupon the ball possession will be changed.

Observations

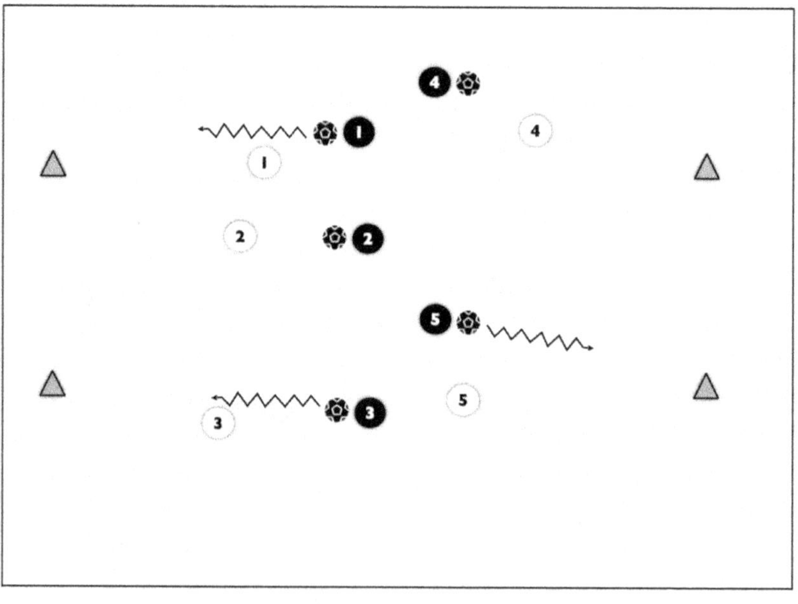

Exercise Nº 27	Main Objective	To improve the dribbling and feint
	Secondary Objectives	To improve the shifting and the lose the mark
Tactical-Technical Means	dribbling, feint, conducting, ball management	
Players	8 (2 teams of 4 players)	Field	20m x 20m (2 squares 5m x 5m)
Material	Cones y balls	Time	2 x 4'
Explanation		

Game 4:4, two squares are marked in the field in which each team places a player. The player with the ball possession scores a goal each time the player inside the squares controls the ball dribbles to his direct opponent before passing the ball, whereupon they will continue with the ball possession.

Observations

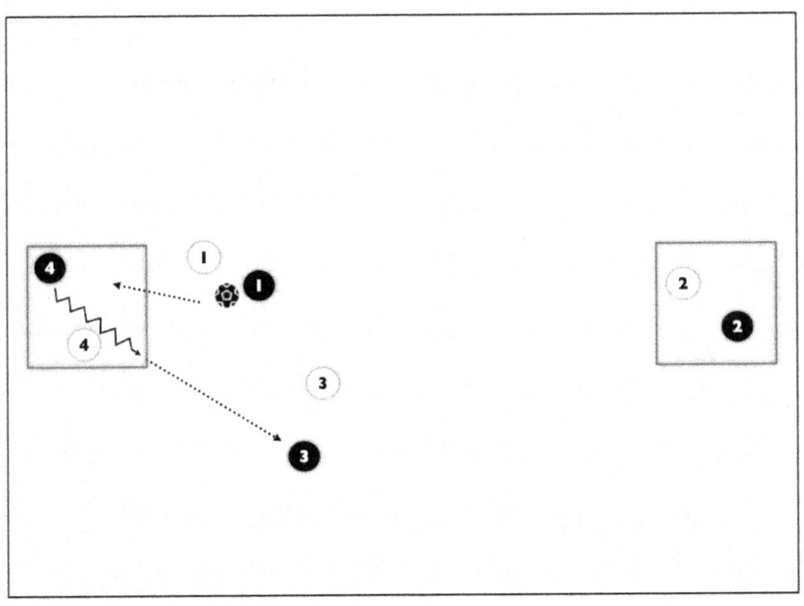

Exercise N° 28	Main Objective	To improve the dribbling and feint
	Secondary Objectives	
Tactical-Technical Means	dribbling, feint, conducting, ball management	
Players	9 (3 couples 1:1+3 defense all-rounders)	Field	20m x 15m (6 goals of 2m)
Material	Cones y balls	Time	6 x 1'

Explanation

Game 1:1+1 all-rounder who goes with the defense player (3 groups). 6 goals of 2m are placed in the playing field, each player attacks and defends 3 small goals (see graphic). The player with the ball possession, to score a goal has to dribble to his direct opponents and cross one of the defended goals, whereupon the ball possession will be changed.

Observations	Change the all-roundres every 1'.

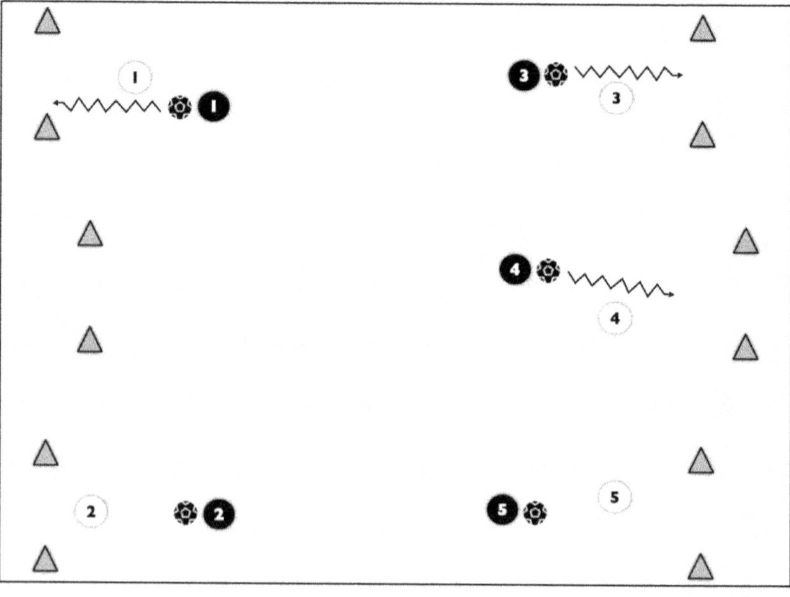

Exercise N° 29	Main Objective	To improve shoot.
	Secondary Objectives	To improve the offensive shifting

Tactical-Technical Means	shot, lose the mark, pass-reception, support, shifting		
Players	5 (2 teams of 2 players + 1 all-rounder)	Field	20m x 20m (2 goals)
Material	Cones y balls	Time	6 x 1'

Explanation

Game 2:1+1 all-rounder who goes with the team with the ball possession. Two normal goals are placed in the playing field which are defended by 2 goalkeepers, each player attacks and defends one of the goals (see graphic). The team with the ball possession has to shot before the fourth pass among its players.

Observations	Change the all-roundres every 1'.

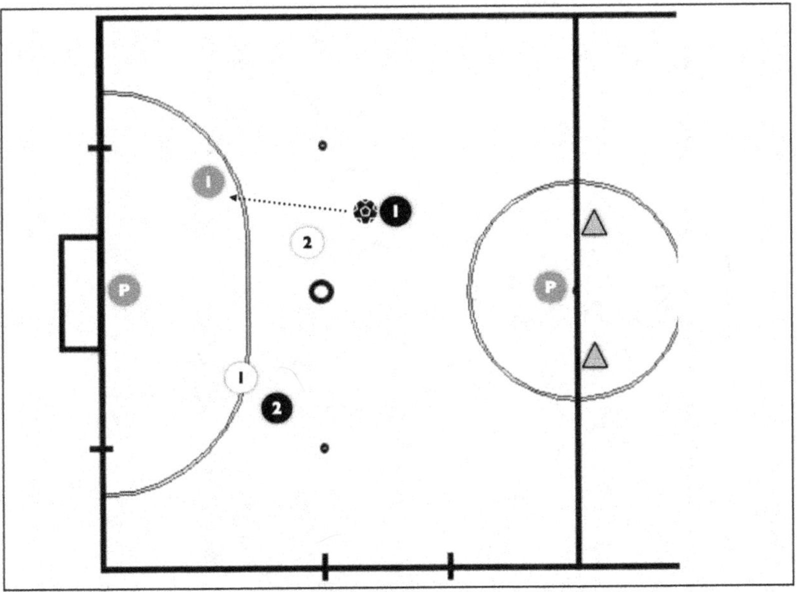

Exercise Nº 30	Main Objective	To improve shoot.
	Secondary Objectives	To improve the positional attack and the shoot.
Tactical-Technical Means	shot, lose the mark, pass-reception, support, shifting	

Players	8 (2 teams of 2 players + 4 all-rounders)	Field	20m x 20m (2 goals)
Material	Cones, ball	Time	12 x 1'

Explanation

Game 2:2+4 all-rounder who goes with the team with the ball possession. Two normal goals are placed in the playing field which are defended by 2 goalkeepers, each player attacks and defends one of the goals (see graphic). The all-rounders are situated in the four corners of the field and support there. The team with the ball possession has to shot before the fourth pass among its players.

Observations	Change the all-roundres every 1'.

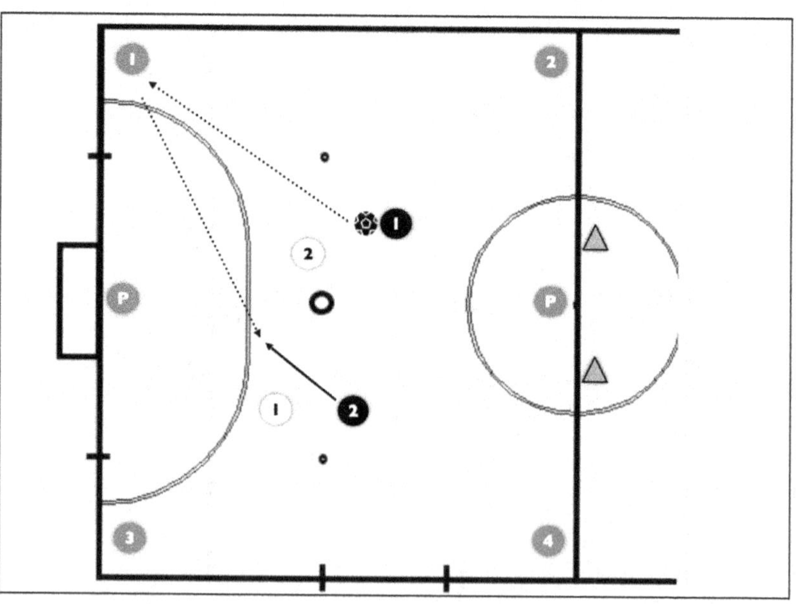

Exercise N° 31	Main Objective	To improve shoot.
	Secondary Objectives	To improve the finalisation

Tactical-Technical Means	shot, lose the mark, pass-reception, support, shifting				
Players	6 (2 teams of 2 players + 2 all-rounders)	Field	goalkeeper's area
Material	Cones, ball	Time	6 x 2'
Explanation			

Game 2:2+2 all-rounder who help the team with the ball possession and support from the edge area (see graphic). Each team attack and defend the same goal. The team with the ball possession only can shot four times before shooting.

Observations	Change the all-roundres every 2'. If the goalkeeper catch the ball, he will deliver it to the opposite team.

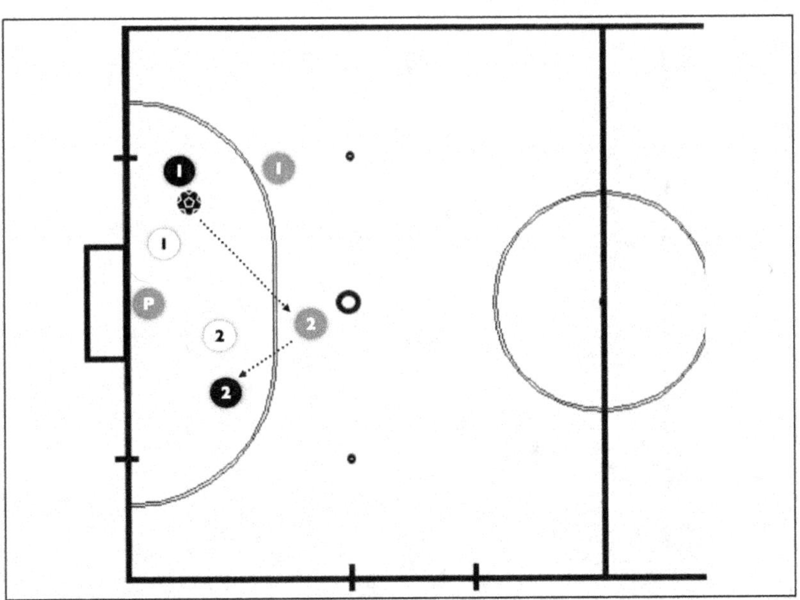

Exercise N° 32	Main Objective	To improve shoot.
	Secondary Objectives	To improve the finalisation

Tactical-Technical Means	shot, lose the mark, pass-reception, support, shifting		
Players	6 (2 teams of 2 players + 2 all-rounders)	Field	20m x 20m
Material	Cones, ball	Time	6 x 2'

Explanation

Game 3:3+2 all-rounder who go with the team with the ball possession and support one by one each sideline (see graphic). Each team attacks and defends one of the goals. The attackers should shoot before the fourth pass.

Observations	Change the all-roundres every 2'. If the goalkeeper catch the ball, he will deliver it to the opposite team.

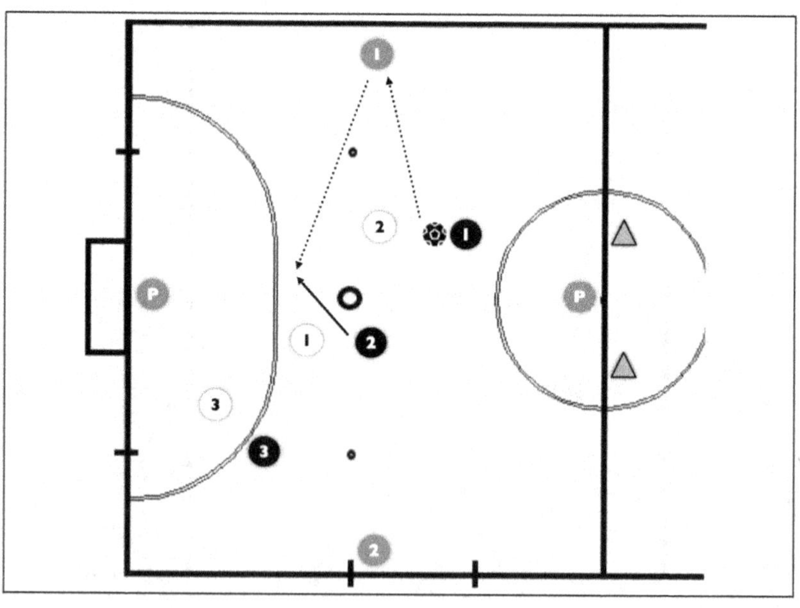

Exercise N° 33	Main Objective	To improve shoot.
	Secondary Objectives	To improve the positional attack

Tactical-Technical Means	shot, lose the mark, pass-reception, support, shifting		
Players	2 (2 teams of 2 players + 4 all-rounders)	Field	20m x 20m
Material	Cones, ball	Time	9 x 1'

Explanation

Game 2:2+4 all-rounder who go with the team with the ball possession and support from the bottom line (see graphic). Two goals with two goalkeepers are situated in the field and each team attacks one of them. The attacker team should shoot before the fourth pass.

Observations	Change the all-roundres every 2'. If the goalkeeper catch the ball, he will deliver it to the opposite team.

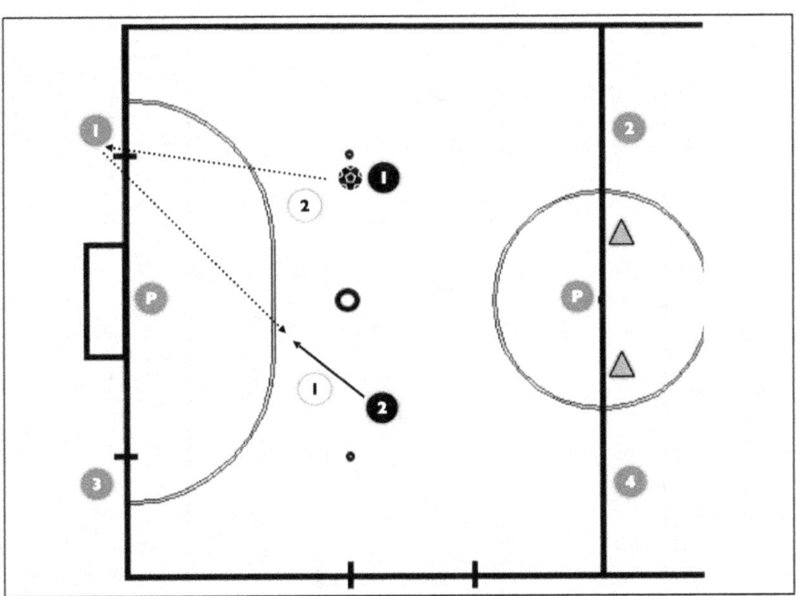

Exercise N° 34	Main Objective	To improve shoot.
	Secondary Objectives	To improve the positional attack
Tactical-Technical Means	shot, lose the mark, pass-reception, support, shifting	

Players	10 (2 teams of 3 players + 4 all-rounders)	Field	20m x 20m
Material	Cones, ball	Time	6 x 2'

Explanation

Game 3:3+4 all-rounder who go with the team with the ball possession and support from the playing field corners (see graphic). Two goals with two goalkeepers are situated in the field and each team attacks one of them. The attacker team should shoot before the fourth pass.

Observations	Change the all-roundres every 2'. If the goalkeeper catch the ball, he will deliver it to the opposite team.

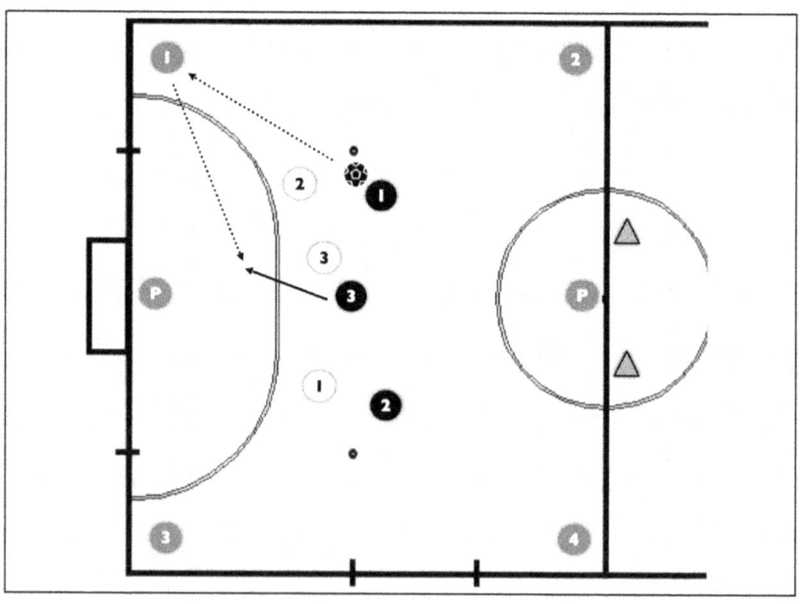

Exercise N° 35	Main Objective	To improve shoot.
	Secondary Objectives	To improve the finalisation
Tactical-Technical Means	shot, lose the mark, pass-reception, support, shifting	
Players	4 (2 teams of 2 players)	Field	20m x 20m
Material	Cones, ball	Time	8 x 1'
Explanation		

Game 2:2, two normal goals with two goalkeepers are situated in the playing field and each team attacks and defends one of them. The attacker team has 20' to shoot.

Observations	If the goalkeeper catch the ball, he will deliver it to the opposite team.

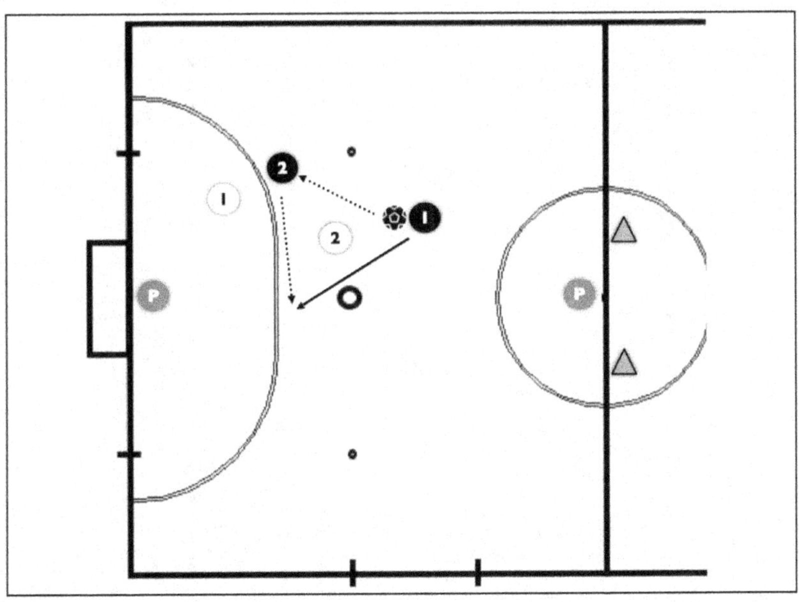

Exercise N° 36	Main Objective	To improve shoot.
	Secondary Objectives	To improve the distant shot
Tactical-Technical Means	shot, lose the mark, pass-reception, support, shifting	

Players	4 (2 teams of 2 players)	Field	20m x 20m (central zone of 10m)
Material	Cones, ball	Time	8 x 1'

Explanation

Game 2:2 with a central marked zone of 10m (see graphic). The players cannot go out of this area and should finish inside the zone. two normal goals with two goalkeepers are situated in the playing field and each team attacks and defends one of them. The attacker team has 15' to shoot.

Observations	If the goalkeeper catch the ball, he will deliver it to the opposite team.

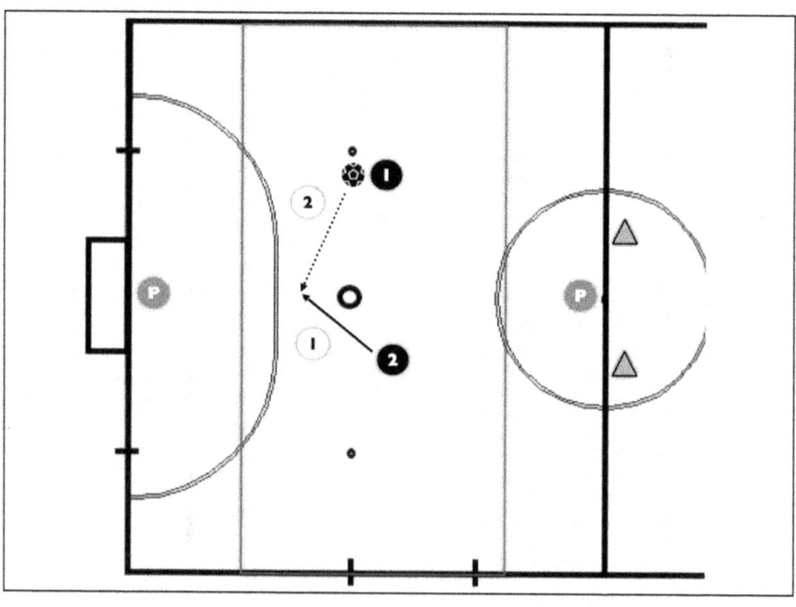

Exercise N° 37	Main Objective	To improve shoot.
	Secondary Objectives	To improve the shifting and lose the mark
Tactical-Technical Means	shot, lose the mark, pass-reception, support, shifting	
Players	6 (2 teams of 3 players)	Field	20m x 20m
Material	Cones, ball	Time	8 x 1'

Explanation

Game 3:3 two goals with two goalkeepers are situated in the playing field and each team attacks one of them. The attacker team has to shoot before the fourth pass.

Observations	If the goalkeeper catch the ball, he will deliver it to the opposite team.

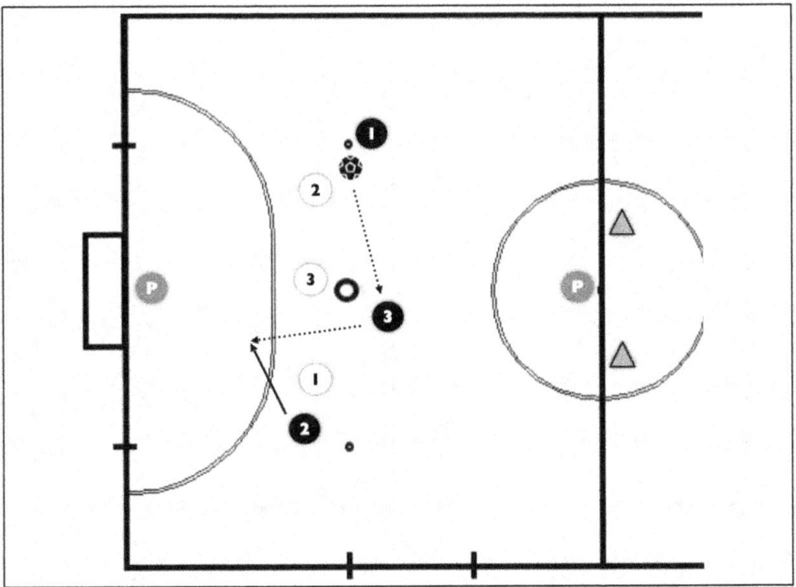

Exercise N° 38	Main Objective	To improve shoot.
	Secondary Objectives	To improve the distant shot
Tactical-Technical Means	shot, lose the mark, pass-reception, support, shifting	
Players	6 (2 teams of 3 players)	Field	40m x 20m (central zone of 20m)
Material	Cones, ball	Time	4 x 2'

Explanation

Game 3:3, a 20m marked central zone is delimited (see graphic) and the game out of it is not allowed, consequently, they should finish in inner zone. Two goals with two goalkeepers are situated in the playing field and each team attacks one of them. The attacker team has to shoot before the fourth pass.

Observations	If the goalkeeper catch the ball, he will deliver it to the opposite team.

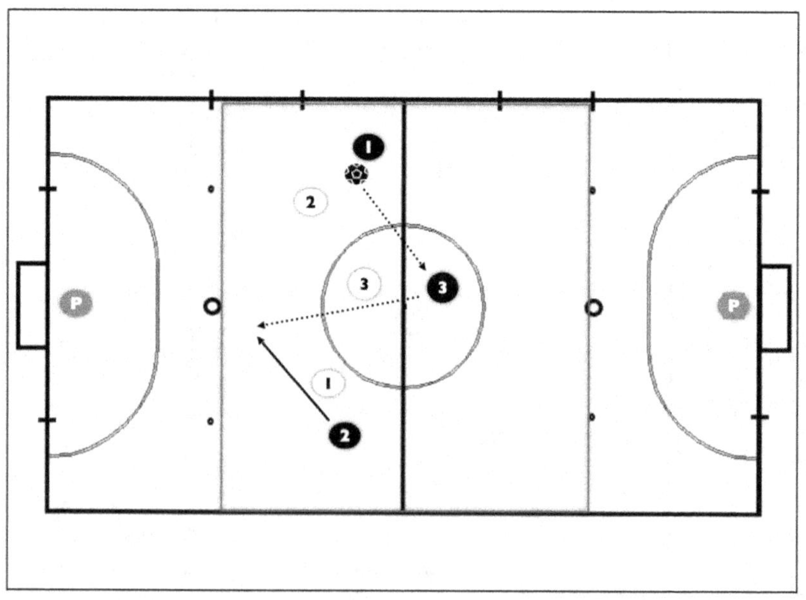

Exercise N° 39	Main Objective	To improve shoot.
	Secondary Objectives	To improve the distant shot

Tactical-Technical Means	shot, lose the mark, pass-reception, support, shifting		
Players	8 (2 teams of 4 players)	Field	40m x 20m (central zone of 20m)
Material	Cones, ball	Time	4 x 2'

Explanation

Game 4:4, a 20m marked central zone is delimited (see graphic) and the game out of it is not allowed, consequently, they should finish in inner zone. Two goals with two goalkeepers are situated in the playing field and each team attacks one of them. The attacker team has to shoot before the fourth pass.

Observations	If the goalkeeper catch the ball, he will deliver it to the opposite team.

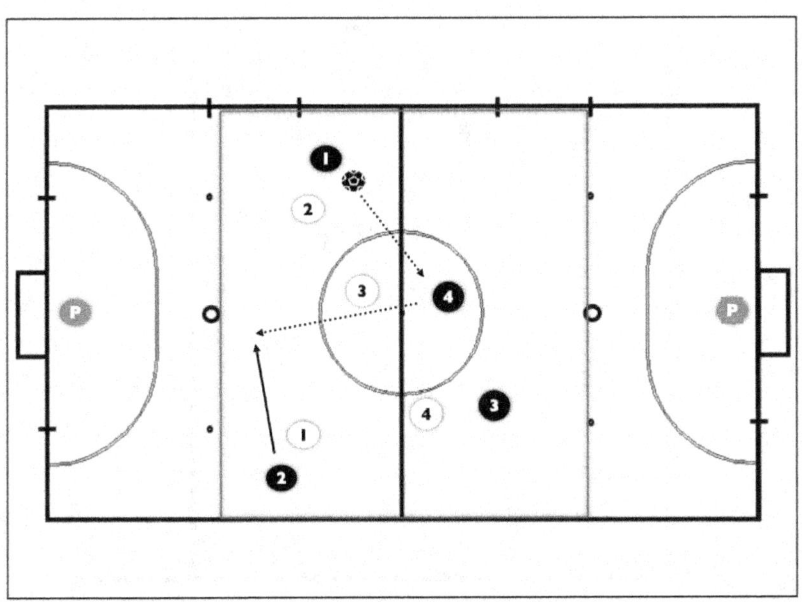

Exercise N° 40	Main Objective	To improve shoot.
	Secondary Objectives	To improve the lose the mark and play a one-two
Tactical-Technical Means	shot, lose the mark, pass-reception, support, shifting	

Players	5 (2 teams of2 players + 1 defense all-rounder)	Field	20m x 20m
Material	Cones, ball	Time	9 x 1'

Explanation
Game 2:2+1 defense all-rounder. Two goals with two goalkeepers are situated in the playing field and each team attacks one of them. The attacker team has 20' to finish the play with a shot.

Observations	Change the all-rounders every 1'. If the goalkeeper catch the ball, he will deliver it to the opposite team.

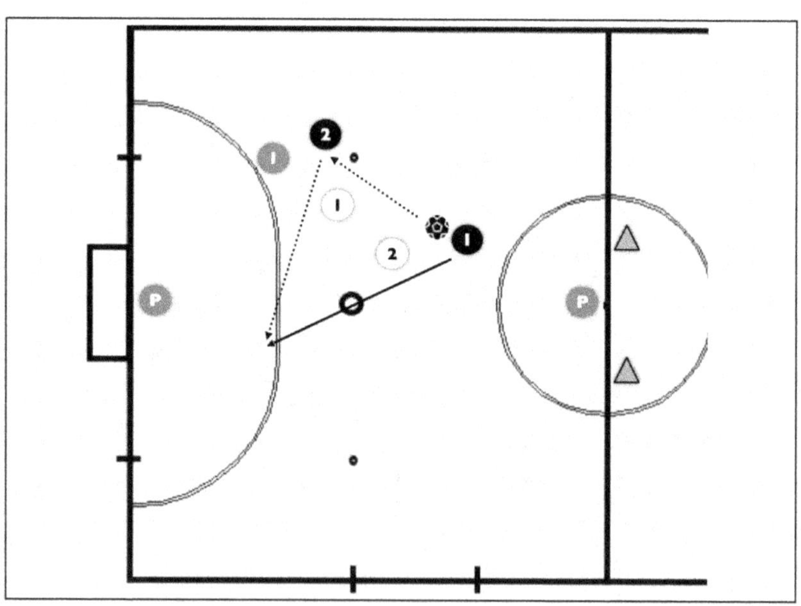

Exercise N° 41	Main Objective	To improve shoot.
	Secondary Objectives	To improve the management
Tactical-Technical Means	shot, ball management, shifting	
Players	3 (1 on 1+ 1 defense all-rounder)	Field	20m x 20m
Material	Cones, ball	Time	9 x 1'
Explanation		

Game 1:1+1 defense all-rounder. An open goal is situated in the playing field, it could be marked in the sides by a neutral goalkeeper. The attacker player has 15' before shooting.

Observations	Change the all-rounders every 1'. If the goalkeeper catch the ball, he will deliver it to the opposite team.

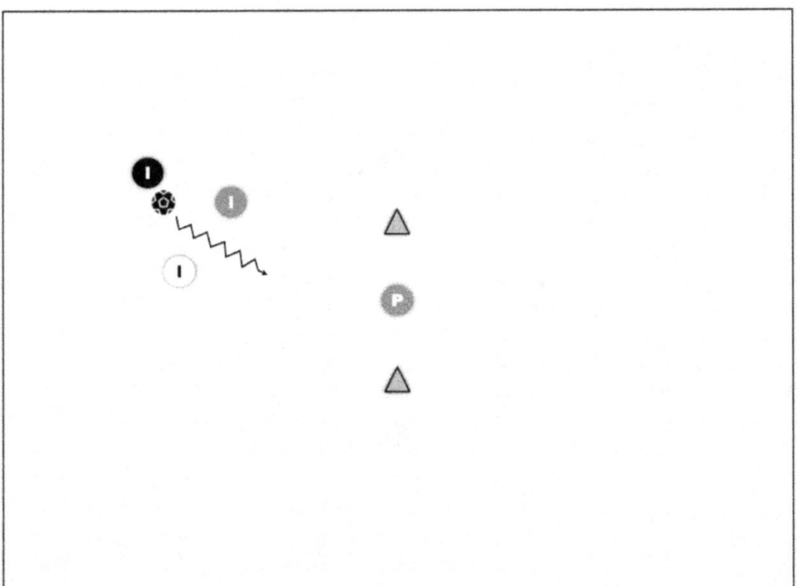

Exercise Nº 42	Main Objective	To improve the header.
	Secondary Objectives	To improve the pass and control.
Tactical-Technical Means	pass-reception, support, ball management	
Players	5 (4 attackers + 1 defense)	Field	8m x 8m
Material	Cones, ball	Time	8'
Explanation		

Game 4:1, the attackers are situated in the square edges and they can move around these edges. The defense is placed in the middle and tries to recover the ball. The attackers only are able to pass the ball with headers, and if they fail they are changed with the defense.

Observations

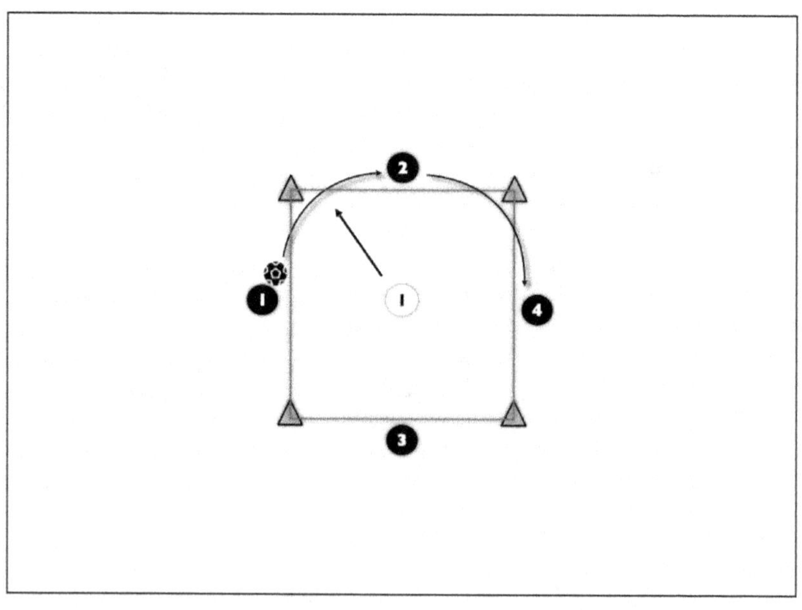

Exercise N° 43	Main Objective	To improve the header.
	Secondary Objectives	To improve the areal control

Tactical-Technical Means	lose the mark, shot, pass-reception, support		
Players	10 (2 teams of 4 players + 2 all-rounders)	Field	20m x 20m
Material	Cones, ball	Time	5 x 2'

Explanation

Game 4:4+2 who support the attacker team. Each team attacks and defends one of the goals. The attackers only are able to pass the ball with headers and, if the ball touches the floor, the ball possession is changed.

Observations	Change the all-rounders every 2'. If the goalkeeper catch the ball, he will deliver it to the opposite team.

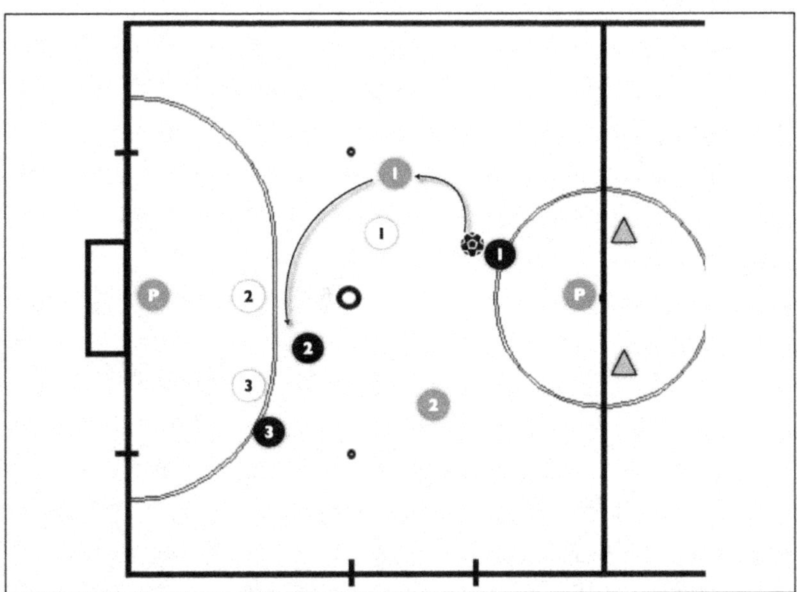

Exercise N° 44	Main Objective	To improve the header.
	Secondary Objectives	To improve the areal control
Tactical-Technical Means	lose the mark, shot, pass-reception, support	
Players	8 (2 teams of 4 players)	Field	20m x 20m (2 goals)
Material	Cones, ball	Time	8'
Explanation		

Game 4:4, each team attacks and defends the two goals turned upside down with 2 goalkeepers. The attacker team is only able to pass the ball and finish the game with headers. If the ball touches the floor or is caught by the goalkeeper, the ball possession is changed.

Observations

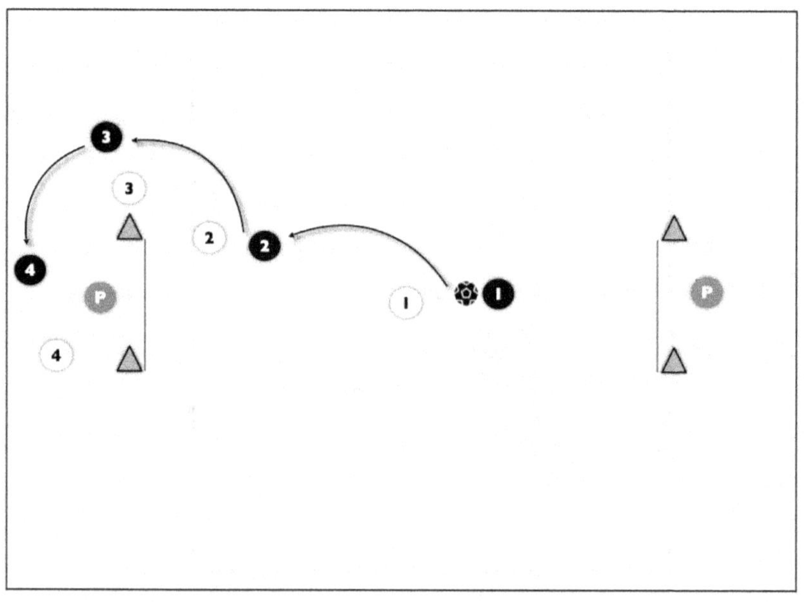

Exercise N° 45	Main Objective	To improve the header.
	Secondary Objectives	To improve the middle from the sidelines
Tactical-Technical Means	lose the mark, shot, pass-reception, support	
Players	8 (2 teams of 4 players)	Field	40m x 20m
Material	Cones, ball	Time	5 x 4'

Explanation

Game 5:5 each team attacks and defends one of the goals with its goalkeeper. Each team places a player in one of the sidelines (see graphic). The goal is only accepted when it comes from a middle and is scored by a header.

Observations

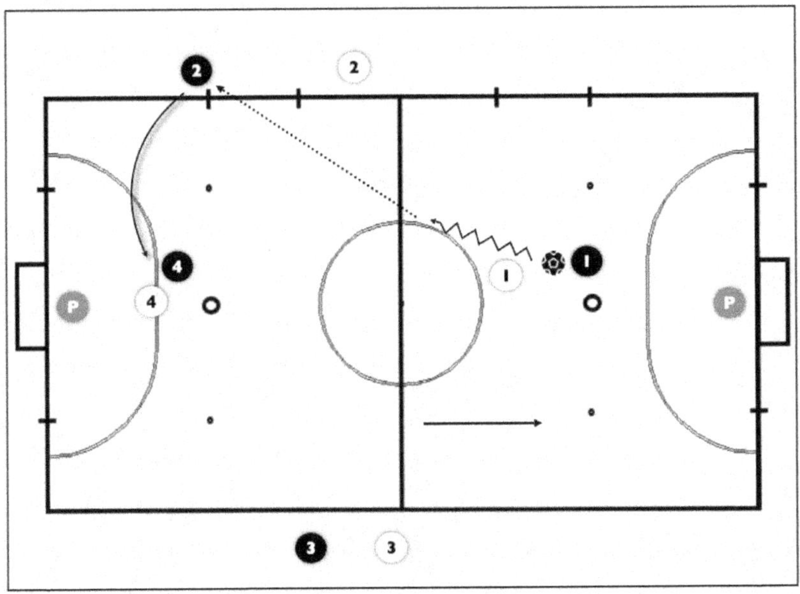

Exercise N° 46	Main Objective	To improve the pass
	Secondary Objectives	To improve support and the support lines

Tactical-Technical Means	pass-reception, support, ball management				
Players	4 (3 attackers + 1 defense)		Field		6m triangle
Material	Cones, ball		Time		8'

Explanation
Game 3:1 with the 3 attackers placed in the triangle corners and the defense tries to recover the ball inside.

Observations	It is compulsory played to one touch.

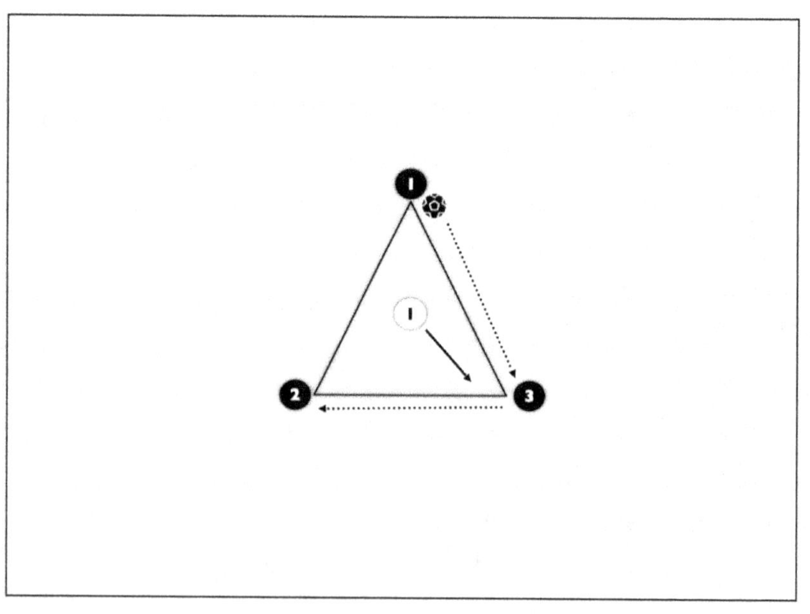

Exercise N° 47	Main Objective	To improve the pass
	Secondary Objectives	To improve the lose the mark and play a one-two
Tactical-Technical Means	lose the mark, pass-reception, support, shifting	
Players	4 (1:1 + 2 all-rounders)	Field	8m x 8m
Material	Cones, ball	Time	8 x 1'

Explanation
Game 1:1+2 who support the player with the ball possession, and they are placed in the square corners.

Observations	Change the all-rounders every 1'. It is compulsory played to 1 touch.

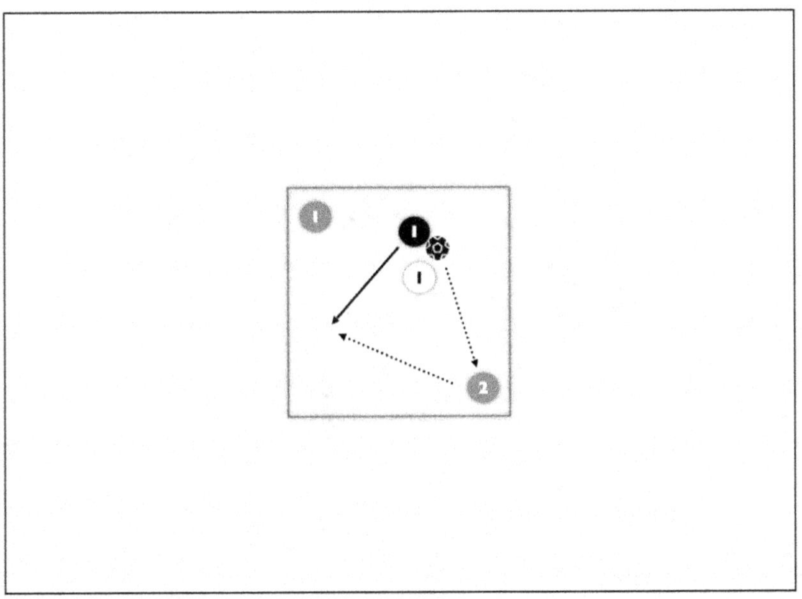

Exercise Nº 48	Main Objective	To improve the pass
	Secondary Objectives	To improve the lose the mark
Tactical-Technical Means	lose the mark, pass-reception, support, shifting	
Players	8 (2 teams of 2 players + 4 all-rounders)	Field	15m x 15m
Material	Cones, ball	Time	4 x 2'
Explanation		

Game 2:2+4 who support the team with the ball possession, and they are placed in the edges of the playing field.

Observations	Change the all-rounders every 2'. It is compulsory played to 1 touch.

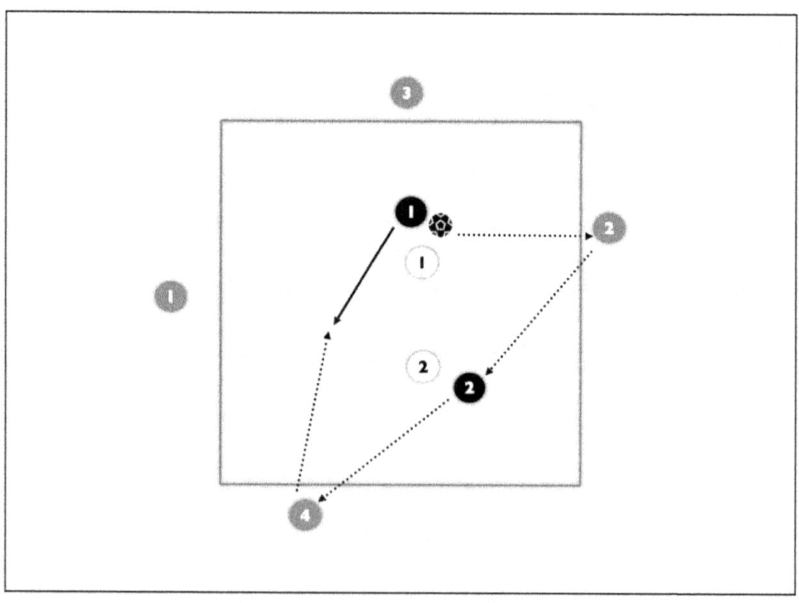

Exercise N° 49	Main Objective	To improve the pass
	Secondary Objectives	To improve the support and the pass lines
Tactical-Technical Means	lose the mark, pass-reception, support, shifting	
Players	9 (2 teams of 3 players + 3 all-rounders)	Field	20m x 20m
Material	Cones, ball	Time	3 x 3'

Explanation

Game 3:3+3 all-rounders who support the team with the ball possession,. The playing filed is divided into three equal zones (see graphic) and 1 player of each team are placed in each zone together with one all-rounder.

Observations	Change the all-rounders every 3'. It is compulsory played to 1 touch.

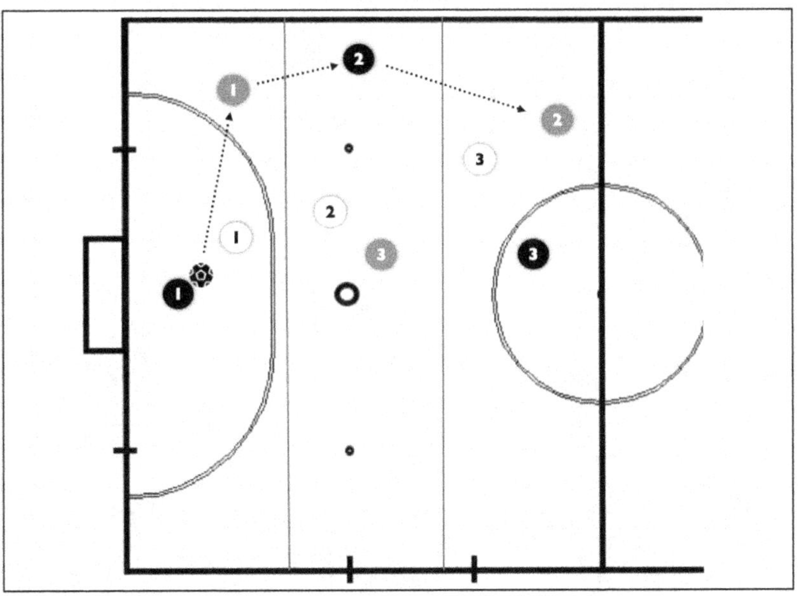

Exercise N° 50	Main Objective	To improve the pass
	Secondary Objectives	To improve the game changes
Tactical-Technical Means	lose the mark, pass-reception, support, shifting	
Players	10 (2 teams of 4 players + 2 all-rounders)	Field	40m x 20m (central zone of 10m)
Material	Cones, ball	Time	3 x 3'

Explanation

Game 4:4+2 all-rounders who support the team with the ball possession,. The playing filed is divided into 2 allowed zones and one forbbiden (central zone of 10m). Each team places half of its players in each zone together with an all-rounder.

Observations	Change the all-rounders every 3'. The attacker team is allow to give as maximum 4 passes before changing the ball to another zone.

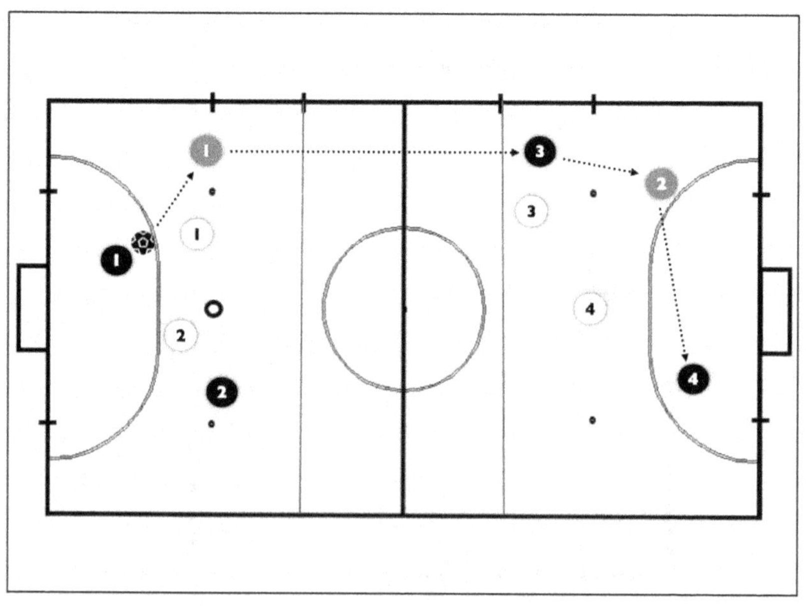

Exercise N° 51	Main Objective	Ball possession	
	Secondary Objectives	To improve the tactical-technical means to keep ball possession	
Tactical-Technical Means	pass, area occupation and ball control		
Players	8 (4:4)	Field	15m x 15m
Material	Cones, ball and bib overalls	Time	4 x 2'
Explanation			

Game 4:4, two of the players of each quartet are situated in two squares. Each quartet tries to give 10 consecutive passes to score 1 point. The players of the squares are changed every 2'.

Observations	

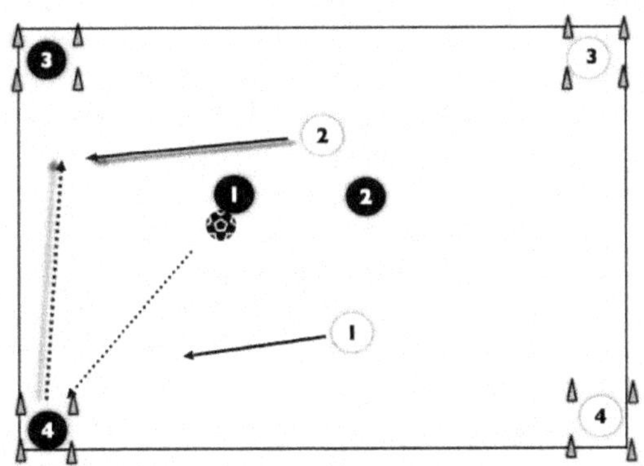

Exercise N° 52	Main Objective	Ball possession
	Secondary Objectives	To improve the tactical-technical means to keep ball possession

Tactical-Technical Means	pass, area occupation and ball control		
Players	8 (4:4)	Field	12m x 12m
Material	Cones, ball and bib overalls	Time	4 x 2'

Explanation

Game 4:4, two of each couple play inside and the other two outside. They have to keep the ball possession to score points, supporting themselves with the two outside players of its own team.

Observations	Positions are changed every 2'. A point is scored every 10 consecutive passes.

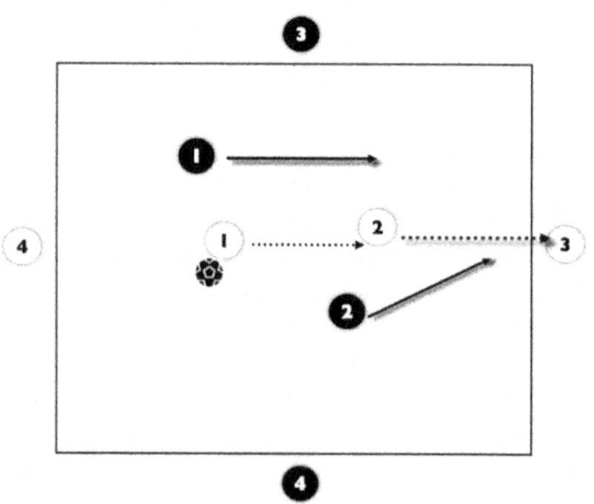

Exercise N° 53	Main Objective	Ball possession and finalisations
	Secondary Objectives	To improve the tactical-technical means to keep ball possession and finalisations
Tactical-Technical Means	pass, area occupation, ball control, ball hitting, dodges, feints and start.	
Players	10 (5:5)	Field	50m x 30m
Material	Cones, ball and bib overalls	Time	10'
Explanation		

Game 6:6, with goals and goalkeepers. They have to give 6 consecutive passes and finish to score a goal.

Observations	The goal will not be acceptable if they do not give the previous needed passes.

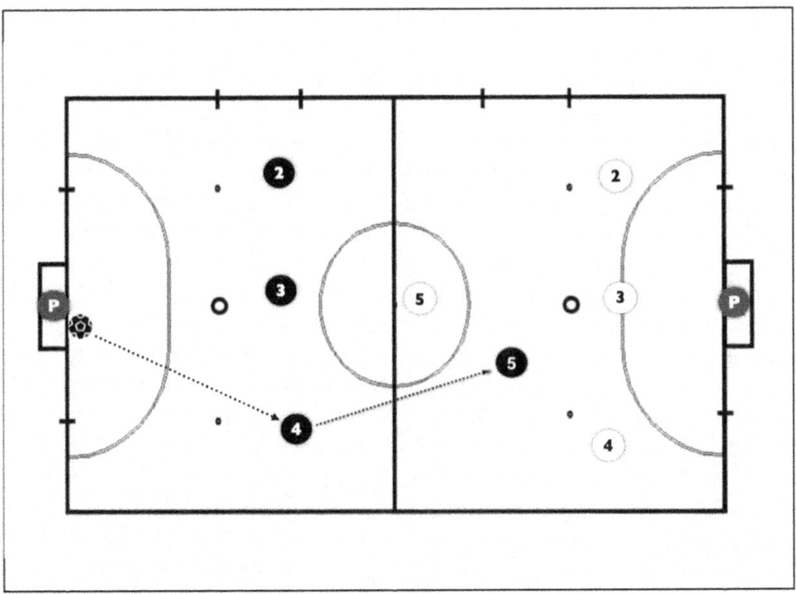

Exercise N° 54	Main Objective	Ball possession and finalisations
	Secondary Objectives	To improve the tactical-technical means to keep ball possession and finalisations
Tactical-Technical Means	pass, area occupation, ball control, ball hitting, dodges, feints and start.	
Players	12 (5:5+2)	Field	50m x 35m
Material	Cones, ball and bib overalls	Time	10'

Explanation

Game 6:6+2, the defense team has two defense all-rounders to make the defense superior.

Observations	They have to give 8 passes at least to score a goal.

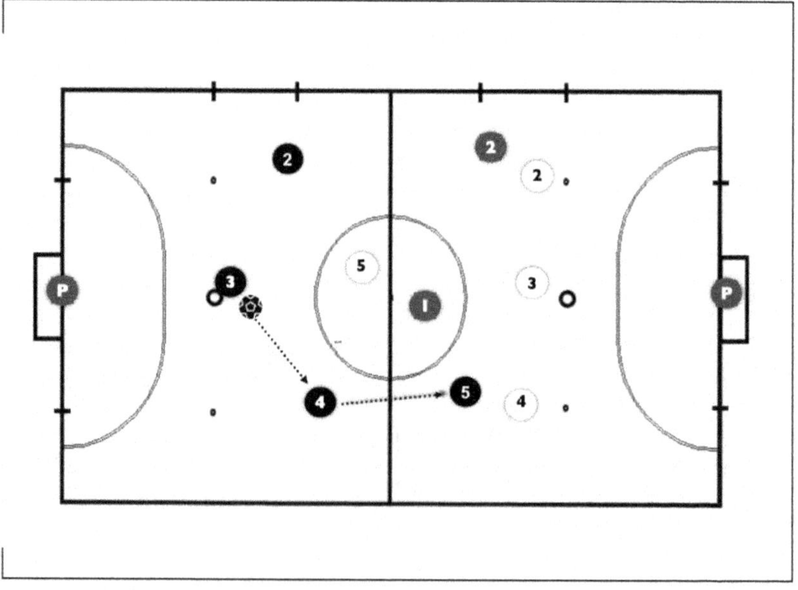

Exercise N° 55	Main Objective	Ball possession
	Secondary Objectives	To improve the tactical-technical means to keep ball possession
Tactical-Technical Means	pass, area occupation, ball control	
Players	12 (5:5+2)	Field	20m x 20m
Material	Cones, ball and bib overalls	Time	10'

Explanation
Game 5:5+2, the defense team has two defense all-rounders to make the defense superior. We have 5 triangles in the playing field and, to score a goal the team with the ball possession should be given a pass inside one of the triangles.

Observations	They have to give 8 consecutive passes at least to score a goal.

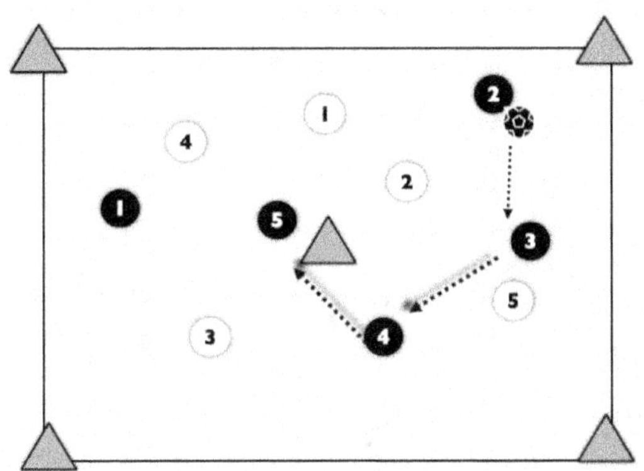

Exercise Nº 56	Main Objective	Ball possession and finalisations
	Secondary Objectives	To improve the tactical-technical means to keep ball possession and finish against the withdrawn opponent.

Tactical-Technical Means	pass, area occupation, ball control			
Players	5 x 5		Field	40m x 20m
Material	Cones, ball and bib overalls		Time	4 x 10'

Explanation

Game 5 x 5, the team with the ball possession has to give 10 consecutive passes to score a goal.

Observations	It has to be given 10 consecutive passes at least to score a goal.

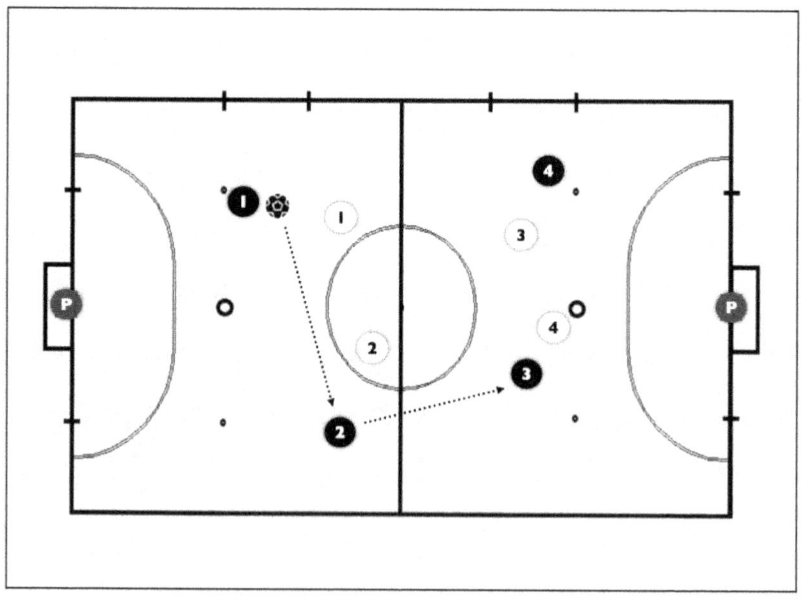

Exercise N° 57	Main Objective	Ball possession and finalisations
	Secondary Objectives	To improve the tactical-technical means to keep ball possession and finish improving the sideline game.
Tactical-Technical Means	pass, area occupation, ball control	
Players	5 x 5	Field	Delimited between 2 zones, one in each sideline.
Material	Cones, ball and bib overalls	Time	4 x 10'

Explanation

Game 5 x 5, the team with the ball possession has to give 10 consecutive passes to score a goal.

Observations	If the ball has not pass through the two sidelines in the same possession, the goal will not be valid.

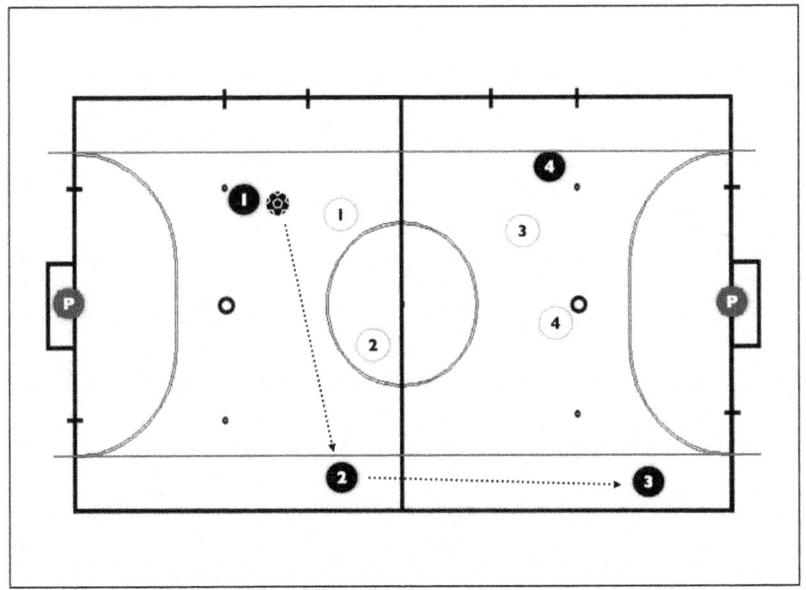

Exercise N° 58	Main Objective	Ball possession and finalisations
	Secondary Objectives	To improve the tactical-technical means to keep ball possession and finish improving the sideline game.
Tactical-Technical Means	pass, area occupation, ball control	
Players	5 x 5	Field	Delimited 10m x 20m zone in the central zone.
Material	Cones, ball and bib overalls	Time	4 x 10'

Explanation
Game 5 x 5, it is delimited a central zone in the playing field where they cannot play, the number of touches is free.

Observations	The delimited central zone cannot be used.

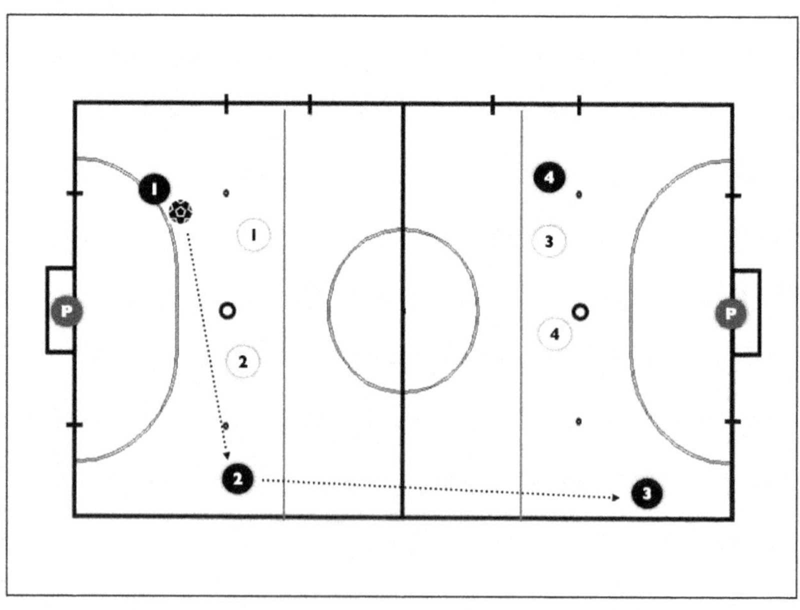

Exercise N° 59	Main Objective	Ball possession and finalisations
	Secondary Objectives	To improve the tactical-technical means to keep ball possession and finish improving the sideline game.

Tactical-Technical Means	pass, area occupation, ball control		
Players	5 x 5	Field	Corner zones of 5m x 5m.
Material	Cones, ball and bib overalls	Time	4 x 10'

Explanation

Game 5 x 5, there are 4 delimited zones in the playing field, to make the goal valid, the ball should come from on of these four zones.

Observations	The ball should come from on of these four zones.

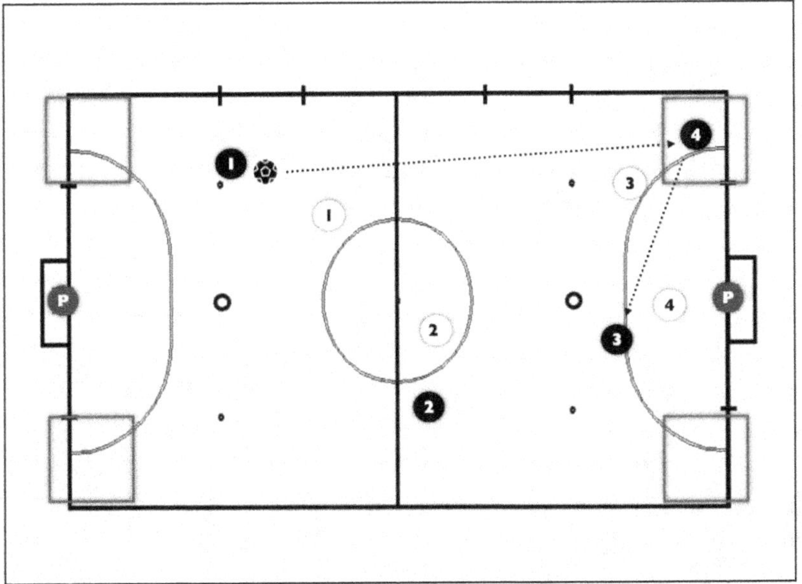

Exercise N° 60	Main Objective	Ball possession and finalisations
	Secondary Objectives	To improve the tactical-technical means to keep ball possession and finish improving the sideline game.
Tactical-Technical Means	pass, area occupation, ball control	
Players	5 x 5	Field	A delimited zone in the central zone of the field.
Material	Cones, ball and bib overalls	Time	4 x 10'

Explanation

Game 5 x 5, in the central field zone there will be a zone in which if there is hand contact of a player from the other team to a player who has the ball in the other team, this will lose the ball possession.

Observations	It has to exist evident contact.

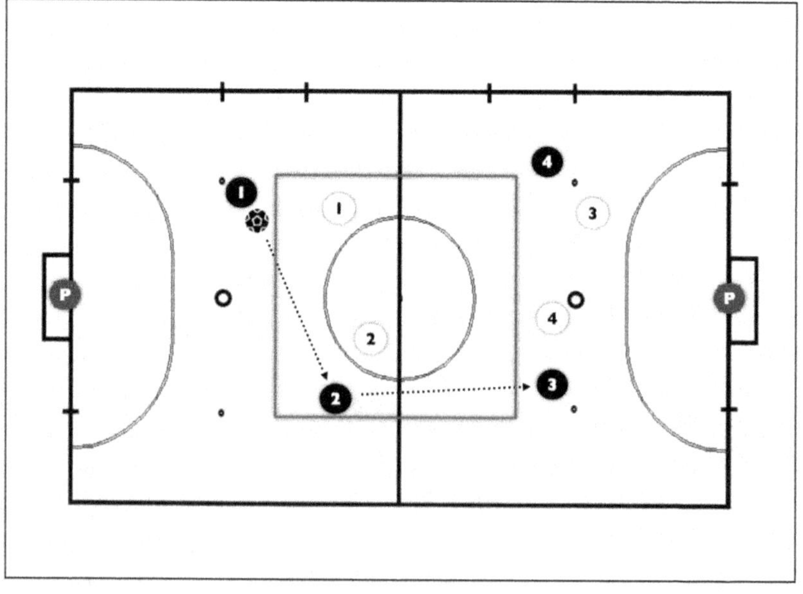

Exercise N° 61	Main Objective	Ball possession and finalisations
	Secondary Objectives	To improve the tactical-technical means to keep ball possession and finish improving the combinatorial game in counterattack.

Tactical-Technical Means	pass, area occupation, ball control		
Players	5 x 5	Field	A delimited zone in the central zone of the field.
Material	Cones, ball and bib overalls	Time	4 x 10'

Explanation

Game 5 x 5, in the central field zone it won't be possible to play the ball. There is a free number of touches and there are offsides rules.

Observations	It has to exist evident contact.

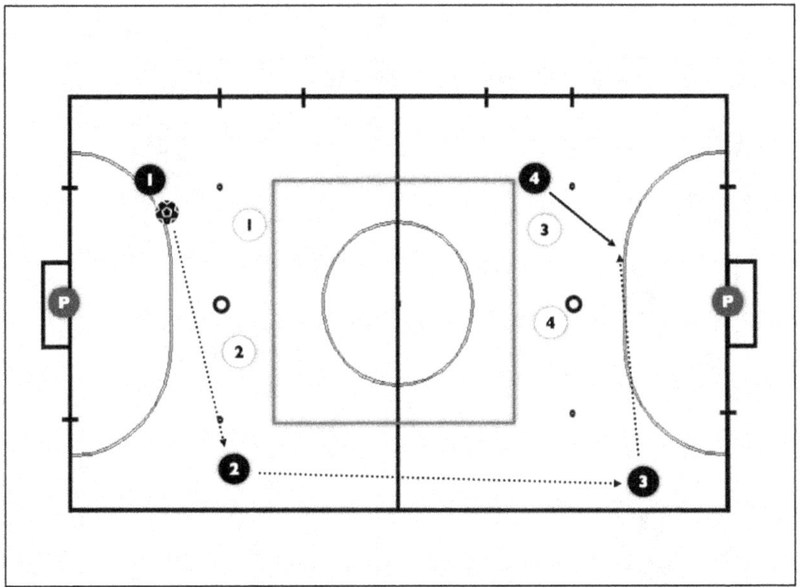

Exercise N° 62	Main Objective	Area ocupations	
	Secondary Objectives	Right functioning of a replacement	
Tactical-Technical Means	pass, area occupation, ball control		
Players	5:5+2	Field	Delimited zone in the edges of 10m x 5m. The playing field will be of 40m x 20m.
Material	Balls and bib overalls	Time	10'
Explanation			

Game 5:5+2, two zones will be set up and each team has to defend one of the marked zones. To score goals, the teams should carry out a replacement in the marked zone of the opposite team.

Observations	The goals only will be valid in the marked zone of the other team.

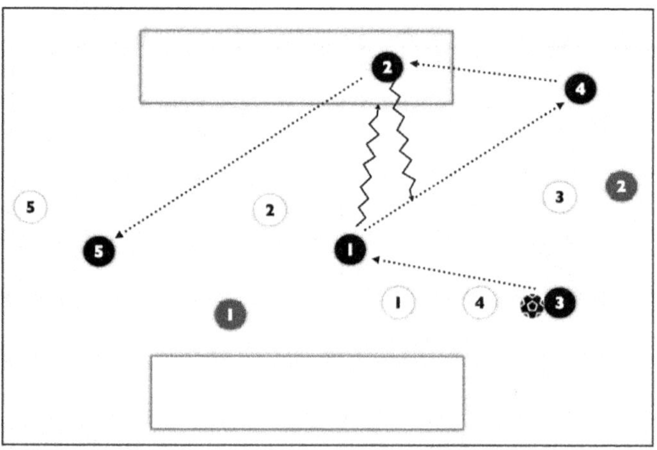

Exercise N° 63	Main Objective	Area ocupations	
	Secondary Objectives	Right functioning of a replacement	
Tactical-Technical Means	pass, area occupation, ball control		
Players	5:5+2	Field	Delimited zone in the edges of 10m x 5m. The playing field will be of 40m x 20m.
Material	Balls and bib overalls	Time	10'
Explanation			

Game 5:5+2, two zones will be set up to carry out the replacements. The all-rounders will go with the team with the ball possession.

Observations	The goals only will be valid if they carry out the replacements properly.

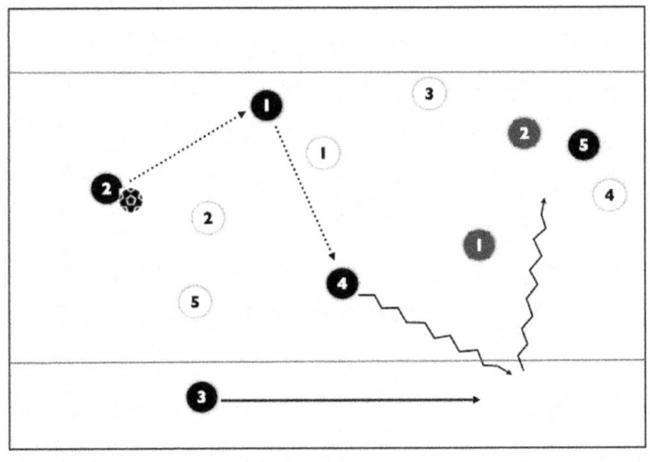

Exercise Nº 64	Main Objective	Area ocupations
	Secondary Objectives	Right functioning of a replacement
Tactical-Technical Means	pass, area occupation, ball control	
Players	5:5	Field	35m x 35m
Material	Balls and bib overalls	Time	10'

Explanation

Game 5:5+2, the player are numberer from 1 to 5. A goal will be scored each time you carry out a replacement with one of your partners with the consecutive number.

Observations	The goals only will be valid if they carry out the replacements properly.

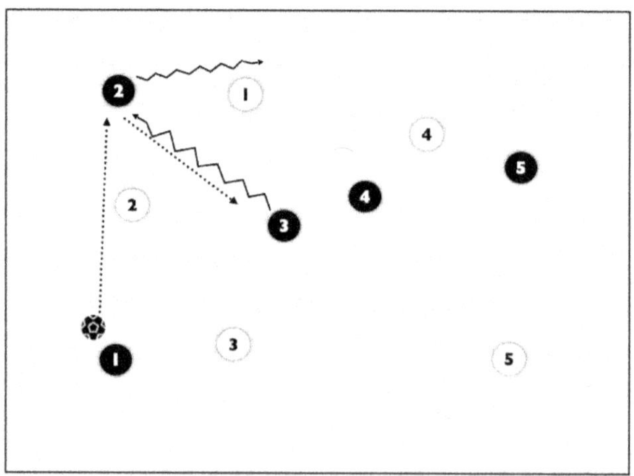

Exercise N° 65	Main Objective	Area ocupations	
	Secondary Objectives	Conduncting technique	
Tactical-Technical Means	pass, area occupation, ball control		
Players	5:5	Field	40m x 25m, 2m goals.
Material	Cones, balls and bib overalls	Time	10'
Explanation			

Game 5:5, two goals are placed. To score a goal, the player with the ball possession should cross conducting the goal.

Observations	The goals only will be valid if they cross conducting the ball.

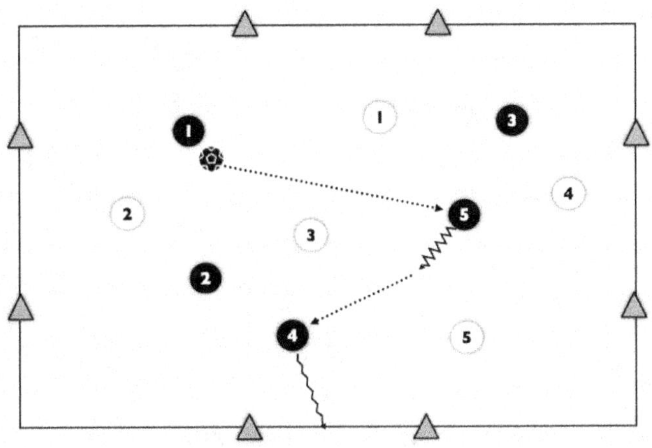

Exercise N° 66	Main Objective	Area ocupations and defensive strategy
	Secondary Objectives	Improvement of ball conducting
Tactical-Technical Means	pass, area occupation, ball control	
Players	6 (two couples) 1:1+1	Field	20m x 20m, 2m goals
Material	Cones, balls and bib overalls	Time	9 x 1'

Explanation

Game 1:1+1, two goals are placed, moreover the defense team has an all-rounder, the attacker tries to overflow the defense and tries to get into one of the goals conducting the ball. Through a robbery the defense scores 1 goal for each robbery. In the same way, the attacker scores a goal for each scored attack. The all-rounders take turns. After the robbery, the defense and attacker team are changed.

Observations	The goals only will be valid if they cross conducting the ball and through robbery to the defense team.

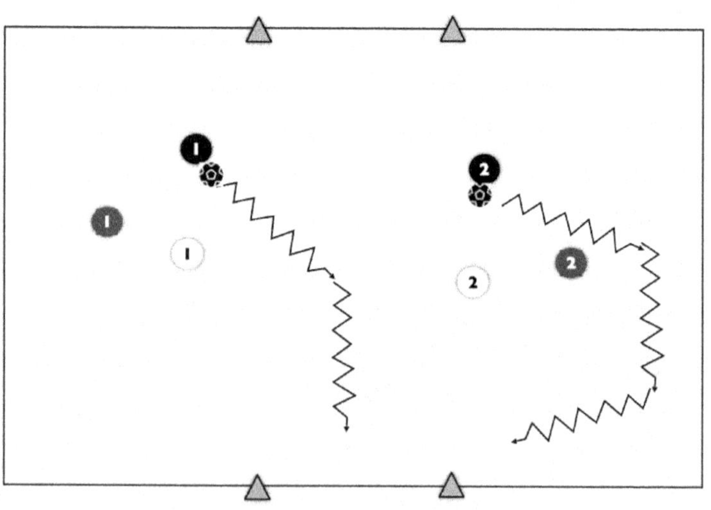

Exercise N° 67	Main Objective	Area ocupations and defensive strategy
	Secondary Objectives	Improvement of ball conducting

Tactical-Technical Means	pass, area occupation, ball control		
Players	9 (three couples) 1:1+1	Field	20m x 20m, 2m goals
Material	Cones, balls and bib overalls	Time	9 x 1'

Explanation

Game 1:1+1, 6 goals are placed, moreover the defense team has an all-rounder, the attacker tries to overflow the defense and tries to get into one of the goals conducting the ball. Through a robbery the defense scores 1 goal for each robbery. In the same way, the attacker scores a goal for each scored attack. The all-rounders take turns. After the robbery, the defense and attacker team are changed.

Observations	The goals only will be valid if they cross conducting the ball and through robbery to the defense team

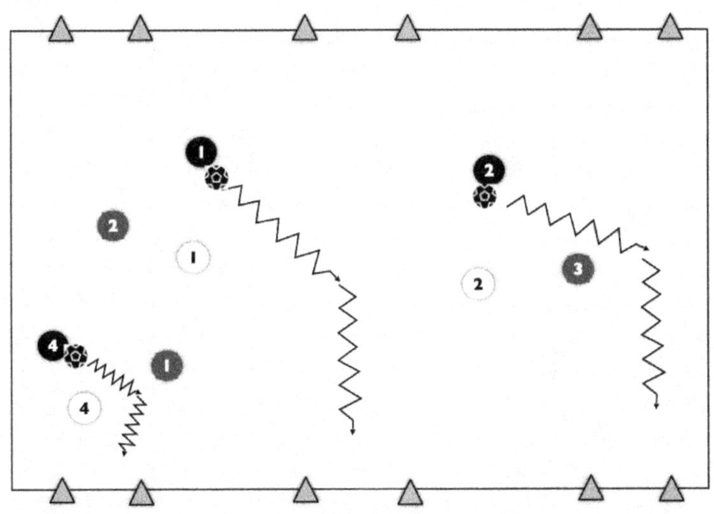

Exercise N° 68	Main Objective	Area ocupations and defensive strategy
	Secondary Objectives	Improvement of ball conducting

Tactical-Technical Means	pass, area occupation, ball control		
Players	6 (two couples) 1:1+1	Field	20m x 20m, 2m goals
Material	Cones, balls and bib overalls	Time	9 x 1'

Explanation

Game 1:1+1, 2 big goals are placed, moreover the defense team has an all-rounder, the attacker tries to overflow the defense and tries to get into one of the goals conducting the ball. Through a robbery the defense scores 1 goal for each robbery. In the same way, the attacker scores a goal for each scored attack. The all-rounders take turns. After the robbery, the defense and attacker team are changed.

Observations	The goals only will be valid if they cross conducting the ball and through robbery to the defense team.

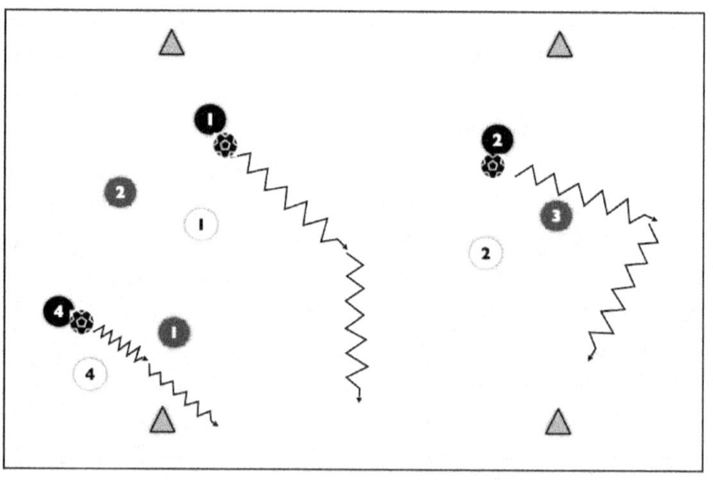

Exercise N° 69	Main Objective	Area ocupations and defensive and offensive strategy
	Secondary Objectives	Improvement of ball conducting
Tactical-Technical Means	pass, area occupation, ball control	
Players	6 (three couples) 1:1	Field	20m x 20m, 2m triangular goals
Material	Cones, balls and bib overalls	Time	8 x 1'

Explanation

Game 1:1, a 2m triangular goal is placed sideways , moreover the defense team has an all-rounder, the attacker tries to overflow the defense and tries to get into one of the goals conducting the ball. Through a robbery the defense scores 1 goal for each robbery. In the same way, the attacker scores a goal for each scored attack. The all-rounders take turns. After the robbery, the defense and attacker team are changed.

Observations	The goals only will be valid if they cross conducting the ball and through robbery to the defense team.

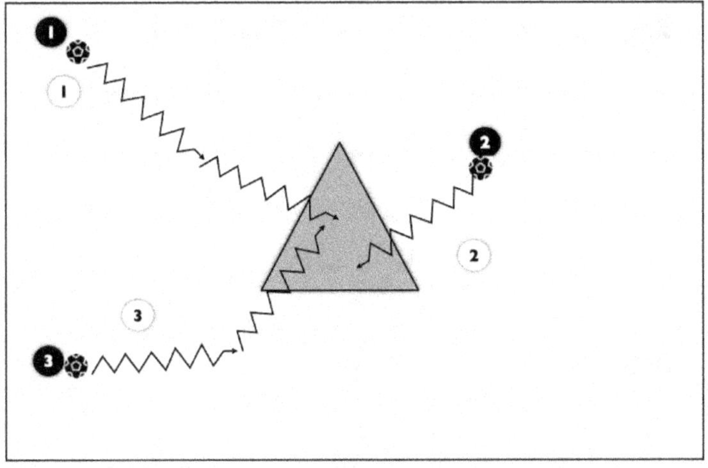

Exercise N° 70	Main Objective	Area ocupations and defensive and offensive strategy
	Secondary Objectives	Improvement of ball conducting
Tactical-Technical Means	pass, area occupation, ball control	
Players	6 (three couples) 1:1	Field	20m x 20m, rectangular 3m goal sideways
Material	Cones, balls and bib overalls	Time	8 x 1'
Explanation		

Game 1:1+1, rectangular 3m goal is placed sideways, the attacker player will be 1' trying to get into the formed goal, and the defense another minute trying to rob the ball.

Observations	Both of them should stay 1' in their position.

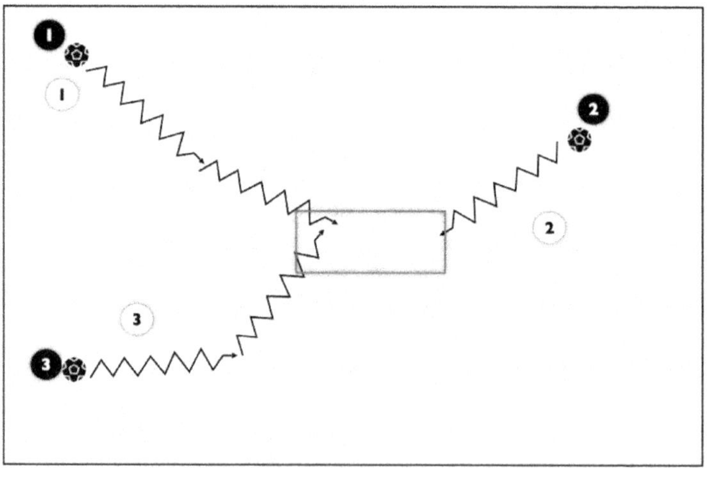

Exercise N° 71	Main Objective	Area ocupations and defensive strategy
	Secondary Objectives	Improvement of ball conducting
Tactical-Technical Means	pass, area occupation, ball control	
Players	6 (three couples) 1:1	Field	20m x 20m, 4 goals of 2m
Material	Cones, balls and bib overalls	Time	8 x 1'

Explanation

Game 1:1+1, 4 small 2m goals are placed, the attacker players should cross conducting the ball in which they will sum 1 goal. The defense should rob a ball to score a goal and pass to the attack.

Observations	The goals only will be valid if they cross conducting the ball and through robbery to the defense team.

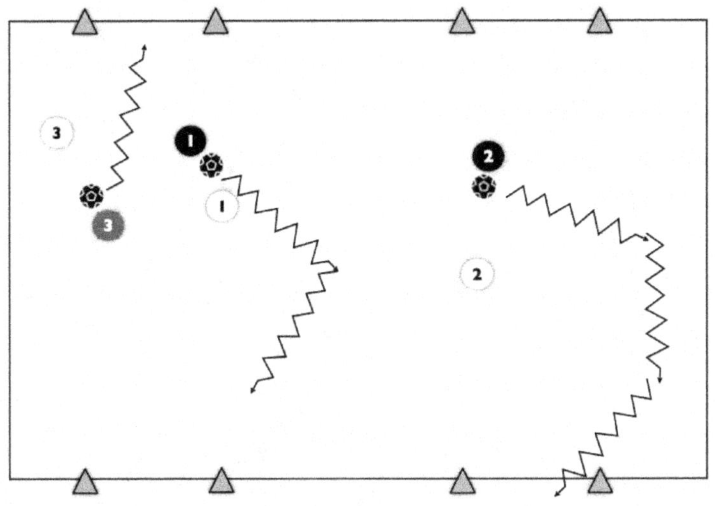

Exercise N° 72	Main Objective	Area ocupation and defensive strategy
	Secondary Objectives	Improvement of ball conducting

Tactical-Technical Means	pass, area occupation, ball control		
Players	9 (three couples) 1:1+3	Field	20m x 15m, two goals of 10m
Material	Cones, balls and blb overalls	Time	9 x 1'
Explanation			

Game 1:1+1, two wide goals are placed, the attacker tries to overflow the defense and cross the goal conducting the ball. The defense would have to rob the ball, thus scoring a goal and passing to the attack. The all-rounders change every 1'.

Observations	The goals only will be valid if they cross conducting the ball and through robbery to the defense team.

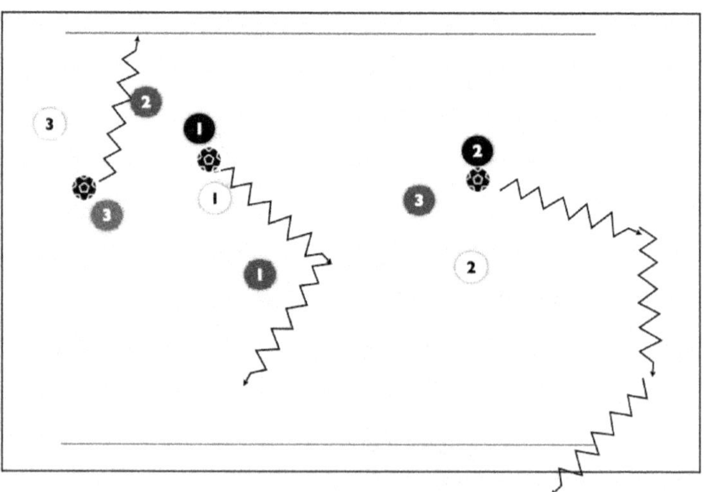

Exercise N° 73	Main Objective	Area ocupation and defensive strategy
	Secondary Objectives	Improvement of ball conducting
Tactical-Technical Means	pass, area occupation, ball control	
Players	9 (three couples) 1:1+3	Field	20m x 15m, two goals of 5m
Material	Cones, balls and bib overalls	Time	9 x 1'

Explanation

Game 1:1+3, two 5m goals are placed. This time the all-rounders play with the team with the ball possession. Each goal is defended by one of the teams. The attacker team to score a goal has to cross the goal conducting the ball. The defense team would have to rob the ball, thus scoring a goal and passing to the attack. The all-rounders change every 1'.

Observations	The goals only will be valid if they cross conducting the ball and through robbery to the defense team.

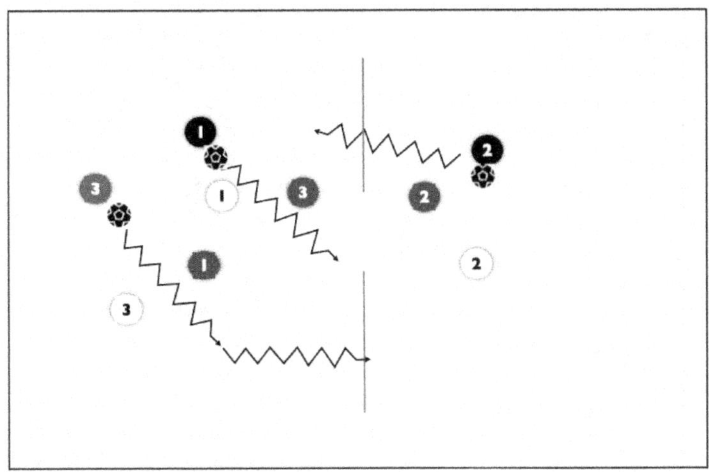

Exercise N° 74	Main Objective	Area ocupation and defensive strategy
	Secondary Objectives	Improvement of area perception and pass
Tactical-Technical Means	pass, area occupation, ball control	
Players	7 (3:3+1)	Field	10m x 10m
Material	Cones, balls and bib overalls	Time	12 x 1'

Explanation

Game 3:3+1, the all-rounders play with the defense team. Two of the players of each team are placed in the field corners and the rest of them and the all-rounder are moving freely by the central zone. The attacker players should keep the ball and the defense try to rob it, after the robbery the possession will be change. The roles are changed every minute.

Observations	The goals only will be valid if they cross conducting the ball and through robbery to the defense team.

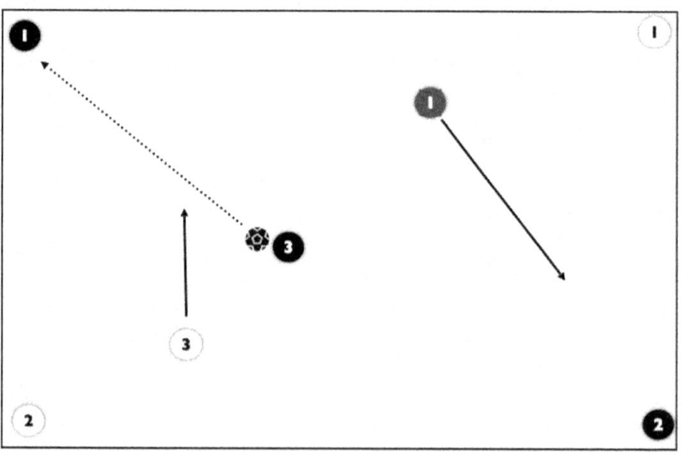

Exercise N° 75	Main Objective	Area ocupation and defensive strategy
	Secondary Objectives	Improvement of area perception and pass

Tactical-Technical Means	pass, area occupation, ball control		
Players	7 (3:3+1)	Field	10m x 10m
Material	Cones, balls and bib overalls	Time	12 x 1'

Explanation

Game 3:3+1, the all-rounders play with the defense team. Two of the players of each team are placed outside the playing field and the rest of them and the all-rounder are moving freely by the central zone. The attacker players should keep the ball and the defense try to rob it, after the robbery the possession will be change. The roles are changed every minute.

Observations	The goals only will be valid if they cross conducting the ball and through robbery to the defense team.

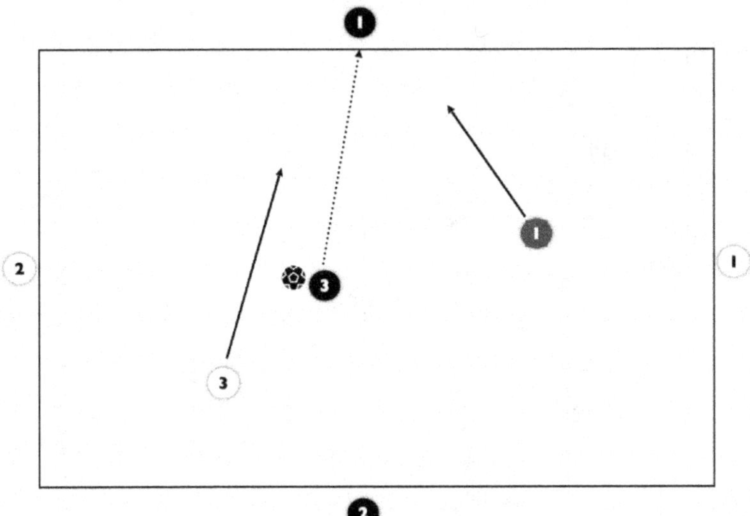

Exercise N° 76	Main Objective	Area ocupation and defensive strategy
	Secondary Objectives	Improvement of area perception and pass
Tactical-Technical Means		pass, area occupation, ball control
Players	10 (5:5+2)	Field	30m x 30m, central zone of 15m x 15m
Material	Cones, balls and bib overalls	Time	7 x 2'

Explanation
Game 5:5+2, 2 of the 5 players of each team are placed inside, their aim is to rob the leaked balls of the central zone. The aim of the team with the ball possession is to keep the ball. Change the roles every 2', and change the defense team and the attacker with each robbery. The all-rounders go with the team with the ball possession.

Observations	The defense will only score goals if he foresees and robs the ball, and the attacker keeps the positions to 2 touches.

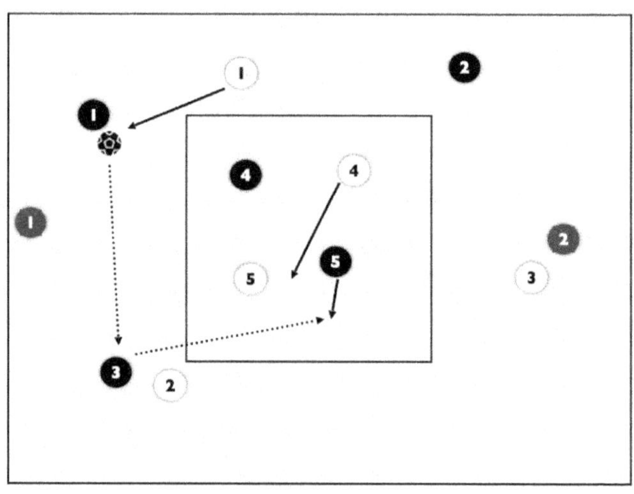

Exercise N° 77	Main Objective	Area ocupation and defensive strategy
	Secondary Objectives	Improvement of area perception and pass
Tactical-Technical Means	pass, area occupation, ball control	
Players	10 (5:5)	Field	12m x 12m
Material	Cones, balls and bib overalls	Time	10 x 1'

Explanation
Game 5:5, each team places 4 players surrounding the outside field and one inside. The defense team will score a goal for each ball the defense team robs inside and pass to the attack. The attacker team should keep the ball possession. The roles will be changed every minute.

Observations	The defense will only score goals if he foresees and robs the ball, and the attacker keeps the positions to 2 touches.

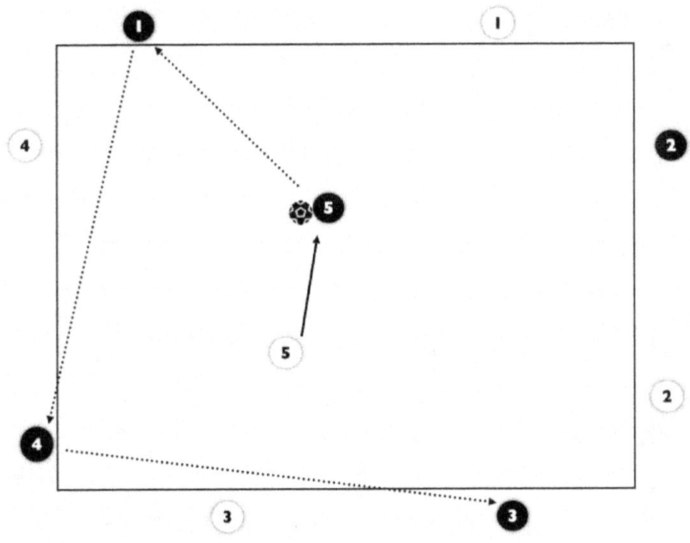

Exercise N° 78	Main Objective	Area ocupation and defensive strategy
	Secondary Objectives	Improvement of area perception and pass
	pass, area occupation, ball control	
Players	8 (4:4)	Field	12m x 12m
Material	Cones, balls and bib overalls	Time	4 x 2'
Explanation			

Game 4:4, each team places 2 players surrounding the outside field and one inside. The defense team will score a goal for each ball the defense team robs inside and pass to the attack. The attacker team should keep the ball possession as much time as they possible. The roles will be changed every 2'.

Observations	The defense will only score goals if he foresees and robs the ball, and the attacker keeps the positions to 2 touches.

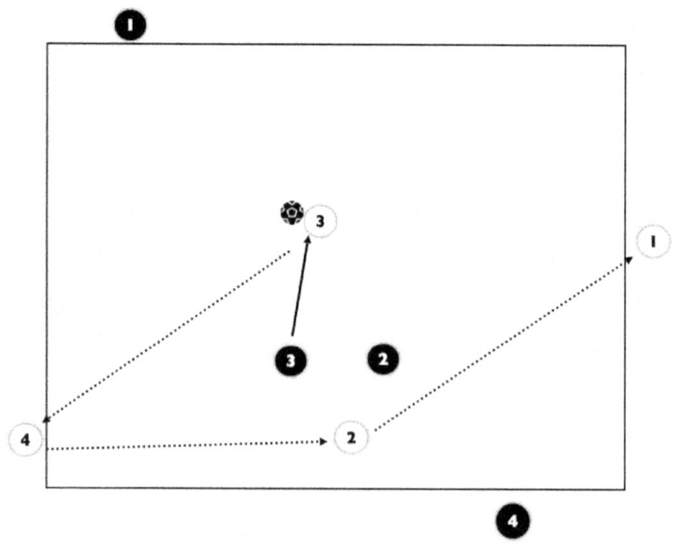

Exercise Nº 79	Main Objective	Area ocupation and defensive strategy
	Secondary Objectives	Improvement of area perception and pass
Tactical-Technical Means	pass, area occupation, ball control	
Players	7 (3:3+1)	Field	10m x 10m
Material	Cones, balls and bib overalls	Time	14 x 1'

Explanation
Game 3:3+1, each team places 2 players in the sides of the field and inside there will be one of each team and the all-rounder who goes with the defense team . The defense team will score a goal each time the inner player foresees and robs a ball inside. The attacker team should keep the ball possession.

Observations	The defense will only score goals if he foresees and robs the ball, and the attacker keeps the positions to 2 touches.

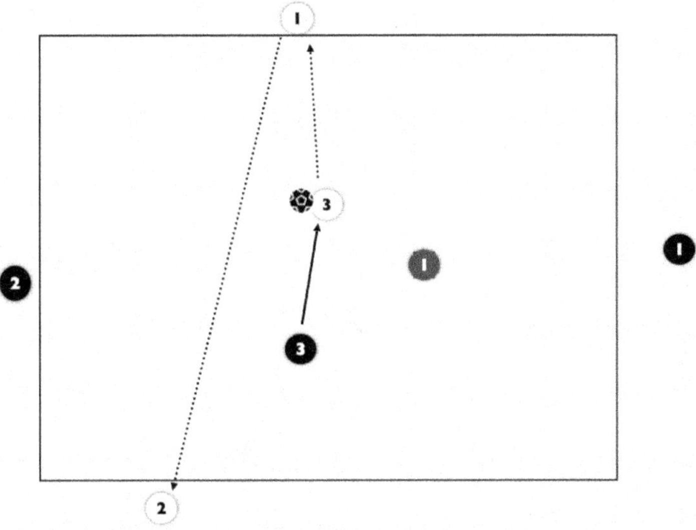

Exercise N° 80	Main Objective	Area ocupation and defensive strategy
	Secondary Objectives	Improvement of area perception and pass
Tactical-Technical Means	pass, area occupation, ball control	
Players	10 (4:6)	Field	20m x 20m
Material	Cones, balls and bib overalls	Time	2 x 4'

Explanation
Game 4:6, the attacker team places 2 players outside the square and 2 inside, and the defense team the 6 players inside the square. The defense team shoul block as much passes as possible while the attackers should try to keep the ball possession. Attackers and defenses has to change every 4'.

Observations	The defense will only score goals if he foresees and robs the ball, and the attacker keeps the positions to 2 touches.

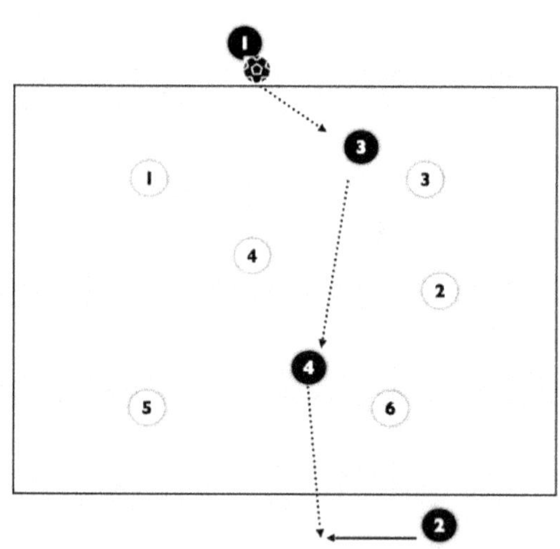

Exercise N° 81	Main Objective	Area ocupation and defensive strategy
	Secondary Objectives	Improvement of area perception and pass
Tactical-Technical Means	pass, area occupation, ball control	
Players	10 (4:6)	Field	25m x 25m
Material	Cones, balls and bib overalls	Time	2 x 4'

Explanation
Game 4:6, the attacker team is located outisde the square while the defense team inside it. The 6 defense try to block as much passes as possible. Change the roles every 4'. Each interception scores a goal.

Observations	The defense will only score goals if he foresees and robs the ball, and the attacker keeps the positions to 2 touches.

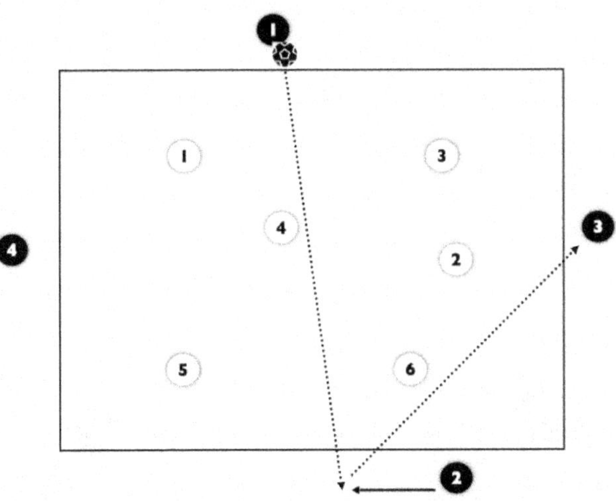

Exercise N° 82	Main Objective	Area ocupation and defensive strategy
	Secondary Objectives	Improvement of area perception and pass
Tactical-Technical Means	pass, area occupation, ball control	

Players	6 (3:3)	Field	15m side triangle
Material	Cones, balls and bib overalls	Time	2 x 4'

Explanation

Game 3:3, inside the triangle, the attacker team is placed in the corners and the defense inside it. They try to block the attacker team balls. We change the roles every 4'.

Observations	The defense will only score goals if he foresees and robs the ball, and the attacker keeps the positions to 2 touches.

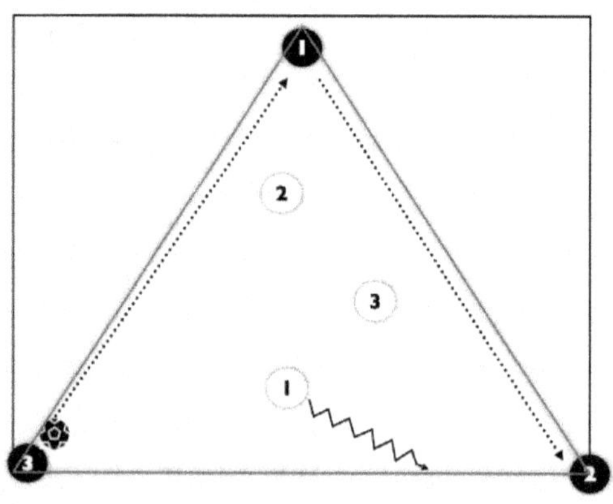

Exercise N° 83	Main Objective	Area ocupation and defensive strategy
	Secondary Objectives	Improvement of area perception and pass
Tactical-Technical Means	pass, area occupation, ball control	
Players	10 (5:5)	Field	12m x 15m side pentagon
Material	Cones, balls and bib overalls	Time	2 x 5'

Explanation
Game 5:5, the attacker team is placed in the pentagon corners and the defense inside it. The aim of the defense team is trying to block as much passes as possible. Roles are change every 5'.

Observations	The defense will only score goals if he foresees and robs the ball, and the attacker keeps the positions to 2 touches.

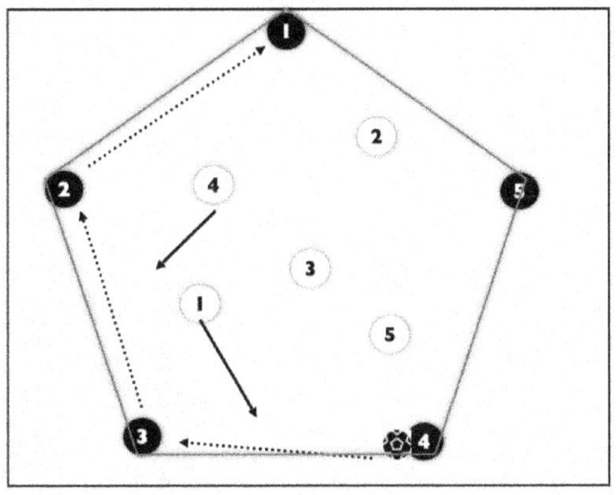

Exercise Nº 84	Main Objective	Area ocupation and defensive strategy
	Secondary Objectives	Improvement of the stopped ball and central areas
Tactical-Technical Means	pass, area occupation, ball control, shot and clearance	
Players	7 (3:3+1)	Field	20m x 30m
Material	Cones, balls and bib overalls	Time	6 x 2'
Explanation		

Game 3:3+1, the all-rounder plays with the attacker team of the opposite team, two of them are situated in the corners and and the third one in the middle. The three defenses are placed inside and their aim is not to let them score a goal. Change the roles every 2'.

Observations	Not to let the attacker team to score a goal.

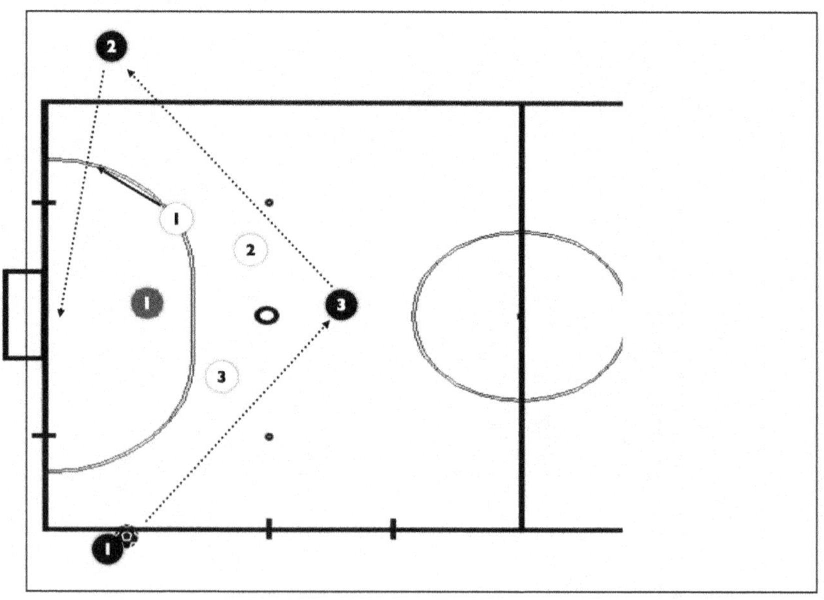

Exercise N° 85	Main Objective	Area ocupation and defensive strategy
	Secondary Objectives	Improvement of the stopped ball and central areas

Tactical-Technical Means	pass, area occupation, ball control, shot and clearance		
Players	7 (3:3+1)	Field	20m x 30m, wide goals of 10m
Material	Cones, balls and bib overalls	Time	6 x 2'

Explanation

Game 3:3+1, the all-rounder plays with the defense team of the opposite team, each team defends one of the goals. The attackers can only score a goal after a finishing previous to a central side of a sideline player and the first touch.

Observations	It's only acceptable the predicted goals of a sideline player pass.

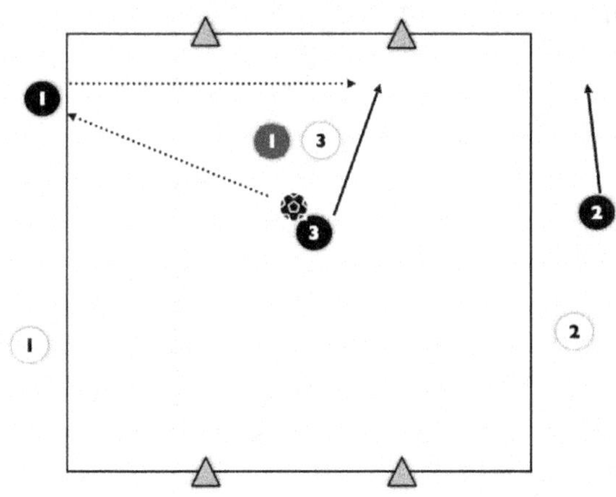

Exercise N° 86	Main Objective	Area ocupation and defensive strategy
	Secondary Objectives	Improvement of the stopped ball and central areas
Tactical-Technical Means	pass, area occupation, ball control, shot and clearance	
Players	5 (2:2+1)	Field	Double penalty area
Material	Cones, balls and bib overalls	Time	9 x 1'
Explanation		

Game 2:2+1, the all-rounder plays with the defense team. A player of each team is situated outiside the area, the attacker can only shoot if it is preceded by a outside player's shoot and always firstly. The defense should try not to have a shoot. There is not goalkeeper.

Observations	It's only acceptable the goals preceding of a sideline player.

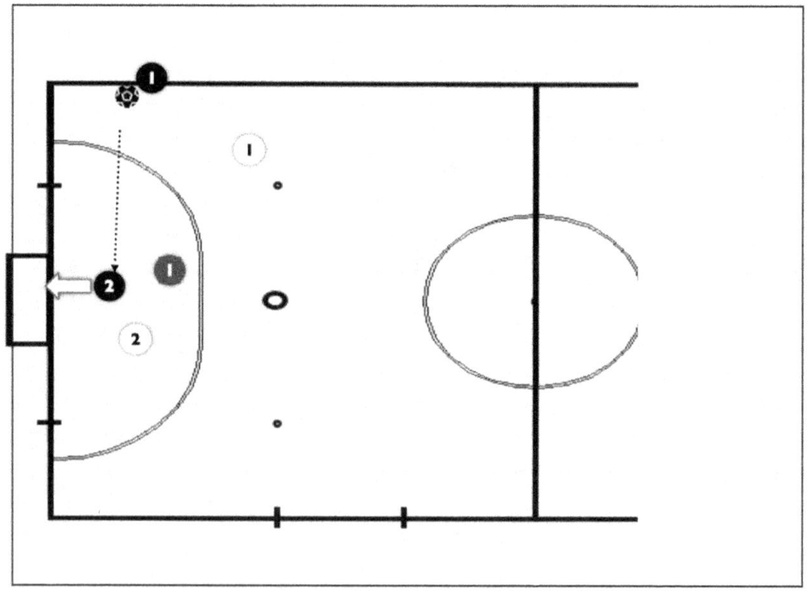

Exercise N° 87	Main Objective	Area ocupation and defensive strategy	
	Secondary Objectives	Improvement of the stopped ball and central areas	
Tactical-Technical Means	Shot and clearance		
Players	2 (1:1)	Field	25m x 25m regulation goalkeepers
Material	Cones, balls and bib overalls	Time	2 x 4'
Explanation			

Game 1:1, each player defends one of the goals, their aim is to clear the rival shot.

Observations	It is not allowed to touch the ball neither with the hands nor with the arms.

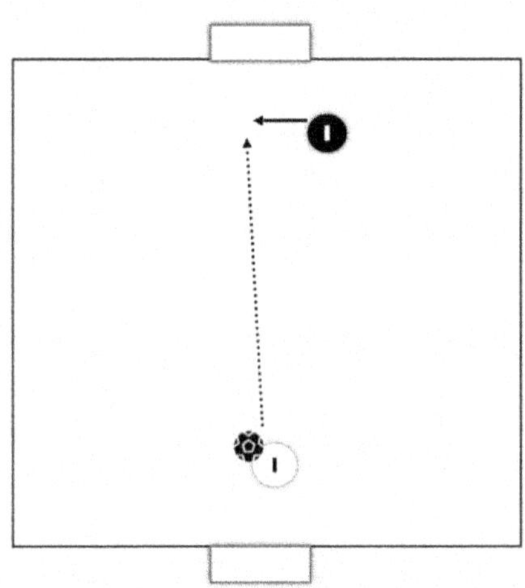

Exercise N° 88	Main Objective	Bodycheck	
	Secondary Objectives	Improvement of hand kickoff	
Tactical-Technical Means	Hand kickoff and bodycheck		
Players	2 (1:1)	Field	25m x 15m regulation goalkeepers
Material	Cones, balls and bib overalls	Time	2 x 4'
Explanation			

Game 1:1, each goalkeeper defends one of the goals and their aim is to block the other player's shot. It is shot with the hands.

Observations	It is shot with the hands.

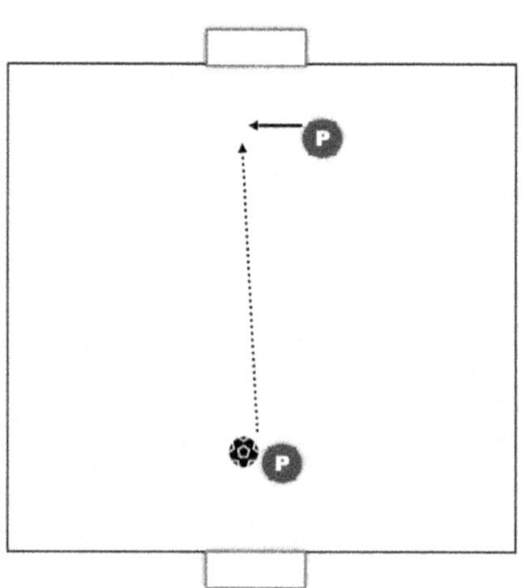

Exercise N° 89	Main Objective	Bodycheck	
	Secondary Objectives	Improvement of leg kickoff	
Tactical-Technical Means	Hand kickoff and bodycheck		
Players	2 (1:1)	Field	25m x 15m regulation goalkeepers
Material	Cones, balls and bib overalls	Time	2 x 4'
Explanation			

Game 1:1, each goalkeeper defends one of the goals and their aim is to block the other player's shot. It is shot with the legs but only to ground level.

Observations	It is only valid the shot to ground level.

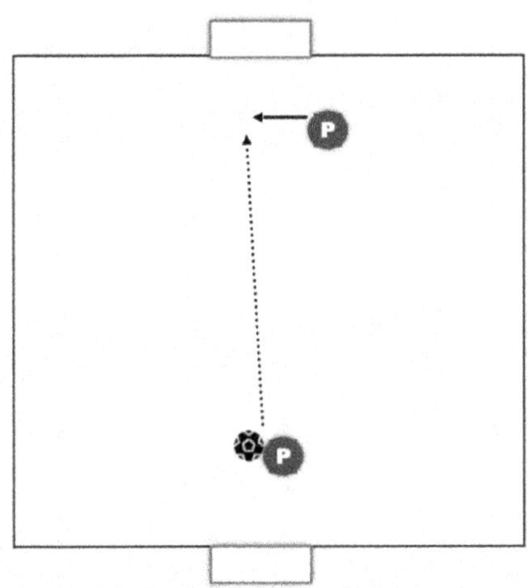

Exercise N° 90	Main Objective	Bodycheck
	Secondary Objectives	Improvement of head kickoff
Tactical-Technical Means	Head kickoff and bodycheck	
Players	5 (4 attackers and 1 goalkeeper)	Field	Penalty area, regulation goalkeepers
Material	Cones, balls and bib overalls	Time	5 x 2'
Explanation		

Game 4 attackers and a goalkeeper, the attackers are placed in the penalty area and they only can shoot by head, through a previous parter's pass, the goalkeeper tries to block the shot.

Observations	It is only valid the shot by head.

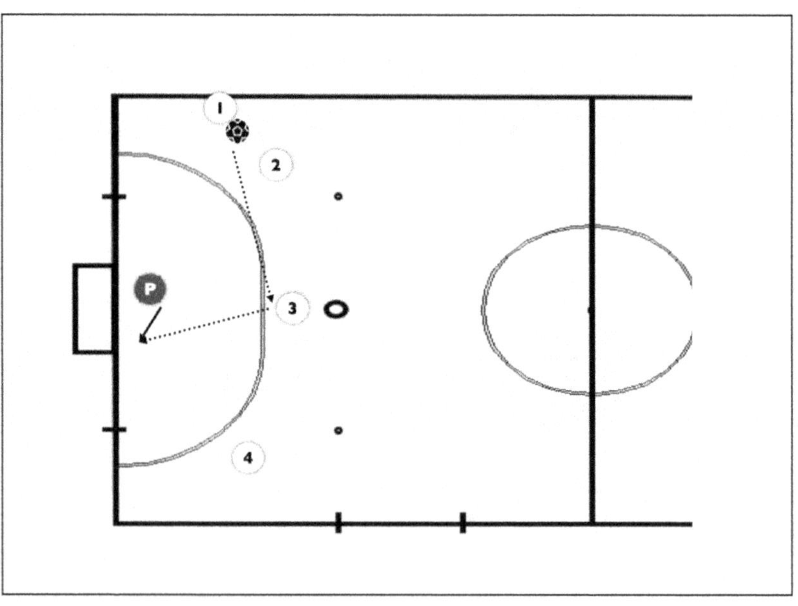

Exercise N° 91	Main Objective	Bodycheck
	Secondary Objectives	Improvement of head kickoff
Tactical-Technical Means	Head kickoff and bodycheck	
Players	8 (3:3 2 goalkeepers)	Field	25m x 15m, a central zone of 5m x 15m is delimited
Material	Cones, balls and bib overalls	Time	10'

Explanation

Game 3:3+2 goalkeepers. The goalkeepers are placed in the central zone and have to block the passes of the 3 players who are situated in each side zone.

Observations — The goalkeepers have to block and retain the ball.

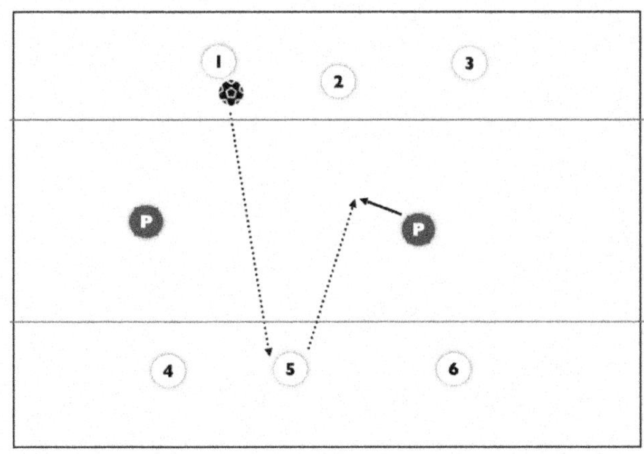

Exercise Nº 92	Main Objective		Bodycheck	
	Secondary Objectives		Improvement of leg kickoff	
Tactical-Technical Means	Leg kickoff and bodycheck			
Players	2 (1:1)	Field	20m x 15m, a 1'50m high net.	
Material	Cones, balls, bib overalls and a net	Time	10'	
Explanation				

Game 1:1 each goalkeeper defends his field avoiding the ball bounce, they have to do it through ball block.

Observations	The ball cannot bounce in own field.

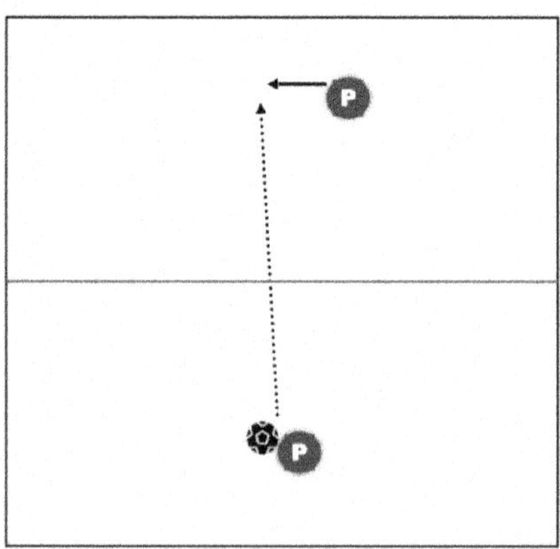

Exercise N° 93	Main Objective		Clearance	
	Secondary Objectives		Improvement of hand kickoff	
Tactical-Technical Means	Hand kickoff and detour			
Players	2 (1:1)	Field	25m x 15m, obligatory goals	
Material	Cones, balls, and bib overalls	Time	5 x 2'	
Explanation				

Game 1:1 each goalkeeper defends his field avoiding the other goalkeeper to hit it with the hands in his goal, and should avoid it by clearing it.

Observations	The ball cannot be touched.

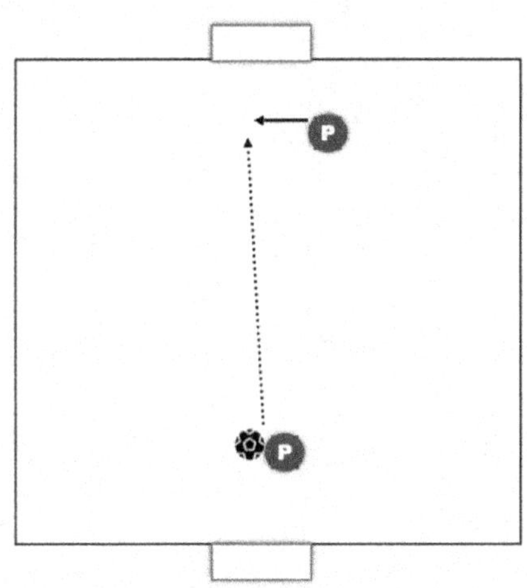

Exercise N° 94	Main Objective	Clearance
	Secondary Objectives	Improvement of leg kickoff
Tactical-Technical Means	Hand kickoff and detour	
Players	2 (1:1)	Field	25m x 15m, obligatory goals
Material	Cones, balls, and bib overalls	Time	5 x 2'
Explanation		

Game 1:1 each goalkeeper defends a goal and his aim is to block the other goalkeeper's shot. It is shot with the legs.

Observations	The ball cannot be blocked.

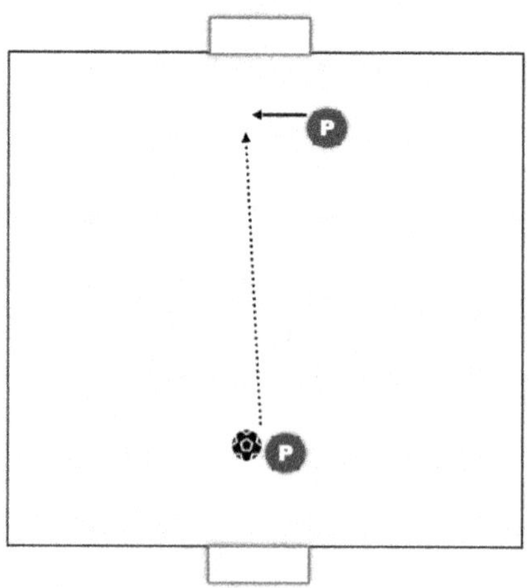

Exercise N° 95	Main Objective	Clearance (goalkeeper)		
	Secondary Objectives	Improvement of the exit technique to detour		
Tactical-Technical Means	Detour			
Players	2 (1:1)	Field		25m x 15m, 1'5m high net
Material	Cones, balls, and bib overalls	Time		8'
Explanation				
Game 1:1 each goalkeeper defends a goal and his aim is to clear with the fists the ball coming from the other goalkeeper and he should try that the ball bounce in the other playing field.				
Observations	The ball should only be cleared with the fists.			

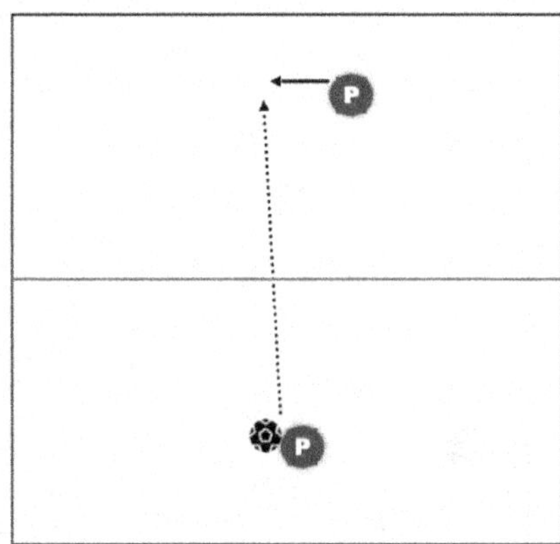

Exercise N° 96	Main Objective	Clearance (goalkeeper)	
	Secondary Objectives	Improvement of the exit technique to detour, middles and head shots	
Tactical-Technical Means	Detour		
Players	8 (3:3+2 all-rounders)	Field	40m x 30m, with two 10m areas
Material	Cones, balls, and bib overalls	Time	6 x 2'
Explanation			

Game 8:8+2 all-rounders, the all-rounders are situated outside and their mision is to carry out central areas of 10m, in the inner field are placed the two teams of 3 where each team has a goalkeeper. The goalkeepers can only clear the ball with the fists and the attackers can only shoot always with head prior to a center of a sideline all-rounder.

Observations	The ball should only be cleared with the fists and shoot with the head.

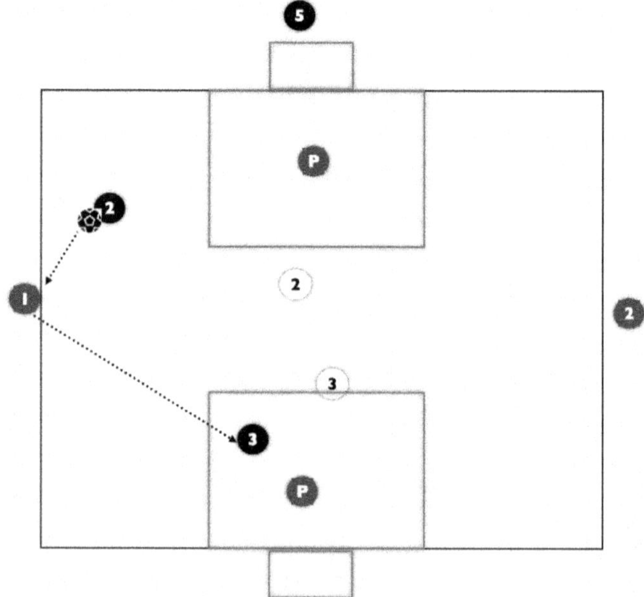

Exercise N° 97	Main Objective	Rebound
	Secondary Objectives	Improvement of the exit technique to rebound and ball shot
Tactical-Technical Means	Detour	
Players	5 (4 attackers and 1 goalkeeper)	Field: 20m x 20m, and a 7m goal.
Material	Cones, balls, and bib overalls	Time: 5 x 2'

Explanation

Game 4 attackers and a goalkeeper, the attackers are placed in the square corners and the goalkeeper in the middle goal. The attackers pass the ball between them until one of them decides to shoot to the goal, the goalkeeper has to rebound the ball.

Observations: The ball should only be rebounded.

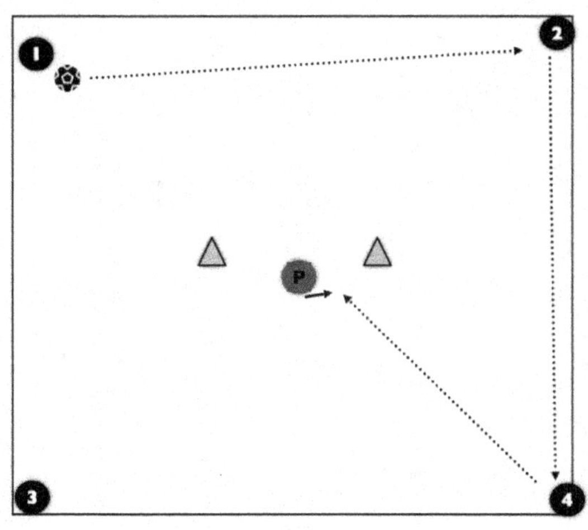

Exercise N° 98	Main Objective	Rebound
	Secondary Objectives	Improvement of the exit technique to rebound and ball shot
Tactical-Technical Means	Rebounds, ball shot and creations and area occupation	
Players	7 (2:2+2 all-rounders + 1 neutral goalkeeper)	Field — 25m x 25m, and a triangular goal of 7m side
Material	Cones, balls, and bib overalls	Time — 6 x 2'
Explanation		

Game 2:2+2 all-rounders + 1 neutral goalkeeper. The all-rounders go with the team with the ball possession who has to shoot before the fourth pass, the defense team has to avoid it and the goalkeeper has to avoid the goal rebounding the ball.

Observations	The ball should only be rebounded and it is not allow to shoot after the fourth pass.

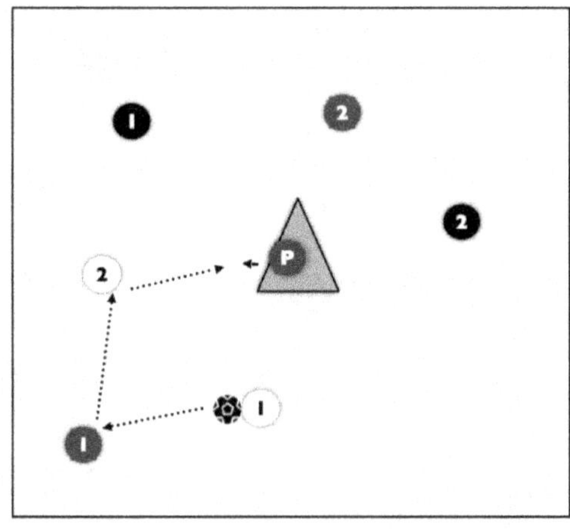

Exercise N° 99	Main Objective	Exits	
	Secondary Objectives	Improvement of the exit technique and ball shot	
Tactical-Technical Means	Exits and dribblings		
Players	2 (1:1)	Field	20m x 15m, and two obligatory goals
Material	Cones, balls, and bib overalls	Time	5 x 2'
Explanation			

Game 1:1, a goalkeeper tries to dribble the other, this one should stop the overflow leaving and trying to take off the ball through an entrance either with the legs or the arms.

Observations	The ball cannot be shot.

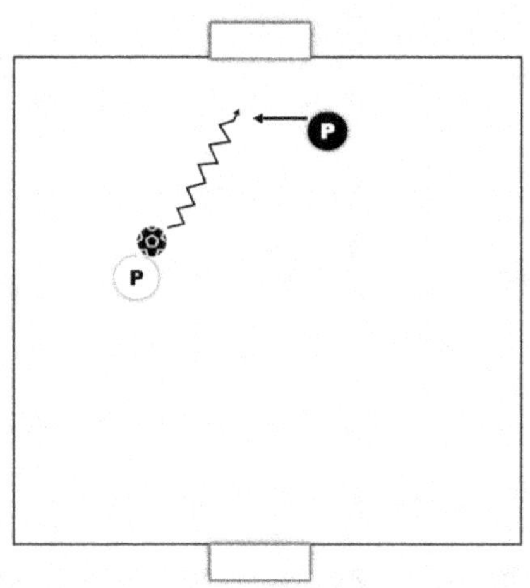

Exercise Nº 100	Main Objective	Exits
	Secondary Objectives	Improvement of the exit technique, ball shot, dribblings and area creation
Tactical-Technical Means	Exits. Dribblings, area creation, pass and ball shot	
Players	6 (3:3)	Field	25m x 20m, and two obligatory goals
Material	Cones, balls, and bib overalls	Time	5 x 2'
Explanation		

Game 3:3, each team defends one of the goals and has a goalkeeper. Each time a fault is made, the affected team has a penalty (penalty zone delimited in the field) where he should try to overflow the goalkeeper. The goalkeeper has to leave and stop it avoiding being overflown.

Observations	It is not allow to shoot in the penalty.

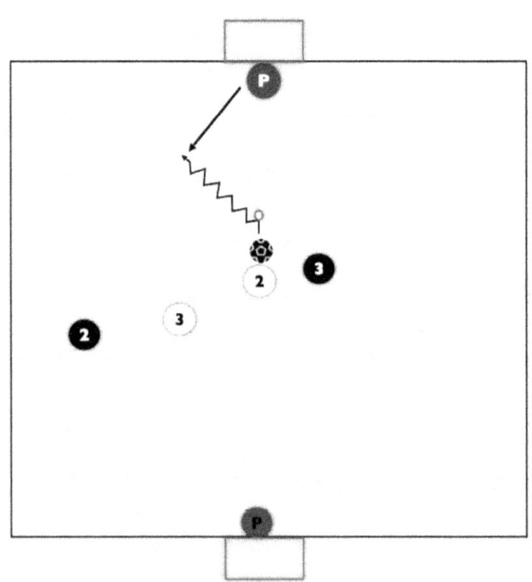